MW00612744

THE UNIVERSITY OF DALLAS STUDIES IN LITERATURE

This series is made possible by a sustaining grant from The Woman's Advisory Board of the University of Dallas.

The Southern Critics

The Southern Critics

An Introduction to the Criticism of
John Crowe Ransom, Allen Tate, Donald Davidson,
Robert Penn Warren, Cleanth Brooks, and Andrew Lytle

LOUISE COWAN

THE UNIVERSITY OF DALLAS PRESS
MCMLXXI

PREFACE

Literary criticism has held an important position in the intellectual spectrum from the time of Aristotle. Its functions, traditionally, have been the explication of texts and the construction of literary theory in order to elucidate meaning. This dual aspect, more or less facing inward toward the literary profession in a technical manner and outward toward an audience in an exegetical one, has developed in recent years into a more forceful penetration of both the technique, and hence the vision, of the artist and the spiritual condition, and hence the psyche, of society. Literary criticism thus takes on a role larger than meditation, becoming in a manner a co-constructor of the work of art; it makes explicit the knowledge that poetry is an active mode of understanding, that it is essential to the well-being of society.

Poetry cannot, as Matthew Arnold fondly hoped, take the place of religion in a world profoundly in need of a sense of the sacred. It cannot by itself produce myth, or symbol, or a sound moral and political order. What it can do — when fully understood and articulated — is to restore human feeling. It can become a discipline for that ordering of the soul that the Greeks called *paideia*. It can open our eyes to the riches of the "world's body" (John Crowe Ransom); can place us in the midst of the "great vital continuum" of human culture (Donald Davidson); can enable us to find "the one lost truth that must be perpetually recovered" — the sense of communion among men (Allen Tate). Poetry and criticism are two sides of the same creative act, both of them performed, as any act of love has always been performed, for all of mankind.

It has been the important accomplishment of the Southern critics to make of literary criticism this reflective, ordering activity which places the imaginative actions of men in a cultural and political context. These writers have made of criticism a moral and spiritual exercise without thereby diminishing the rigor of intellection required for the proper study of poetics. One could conceivably maintain that if we look toward literature with any degree of hope in our time — hope for its reaching more than a small elite, hope for its attaining any sort of moral earnestness, hope for its once more expressing in high imaginative form the enduring virtues of people — then the work of the Southern Fugitive-Agrarians is a necessary knowledge: an opening, a door.

This small book means simply to introduce them to those who do not know them. I have concentrated on the three founders of the school — Ransom, Tate, and Davidson — because it was in their minds and imaginations that the movement took form. Certainly Davidson is less well known than his famous pupils Cleanth Brooks and Robert Penn Warren; and any history of literary criticism would accord these latter men the greater attention. But mine is a brief survey of the foundation of a school of thought that makes up a powerful corrective to our times. Ransom, Davidson, and Tate are the originators of this movement.

Louise Cowan

The University of Dallas
November, 1971

Louise Cowan is author of *The Fugitive Group: a Literary History,* an account of the formation and early years of the Fugitive poets.

The Southern Critics

THE SOUTHERN CRITICS

A volume of criticism published by John Crowe Ransom in 1941 announced a "new" criticism and went to some pains to explore its range. "In depth and precision at once it is beyond all earlier criticism in our language," Ransom declared. "It is a new criticism, and it has already some unity of method." (*The New Criticism*, p. x) He considered its most fundamental pattern to be "criticism of the structural properties of poetry," which, he contended, differ ontologically (that is, essentially, in their very nature) from structures in scientific discourse. Ransom devoted a major portion of his book to an analysis of three very dissimilar critics – I. A. Richards, T. S. Eliot, and Yvor Winters; and though he designated them respectively as psychological, historical, and logical in their dominant interests he nonetheless presented each as a practitioner of the new mode of literary study. In so doing Ransom indicated that the new criticism, as he saw it, stemmed not from a single system of thought but from a unique and original way of regarding the literary object.

Ransom's term – the New Criticism – caught on and became a · label to be used with some lack of discrimination. As Malcolm Cowley has pointed out, virtually every important modern critic has at some time been classified as a New Critic. (*The Literary Situation*, p. 12) It has become the fashion by now, in many quarters, to disparage the entire movement by maintaining that it

never existed – that it was a kind of myth or mystique –
or that it was exaggerated in its importance and, as an
intellectual fad, has exhausted itself. The truth of the
matter is that it was never a program or a school of
criticism; rather, it came about much as any pervasive shift
in intellectual outlook does: as the result of a new
epistemology affecting an established body of thought. As
a new way of looking at a poem, it made itself felt as a
general revolt against the dominant literary tendencies in
the early twentieth century: outside the universities
romantic impressionism dominated the journals; and,
inside, historical scholarship bolstered its absolute au-
thority by an appearance of objectivity borrowed from
the natural sciences.

For a time, then, the New Critical movement was
regarded by its detractors as a kind of conspiracy, fostering
an irresponsible latitude in the study of literature,
encouraging its practitioners to view a poem "in a
vacuum," without recourse to valid literary scholarship.
Disapproval centered on the work of two groups of literary
innovators: in England, beginning in the 1910's, T. E.
Hulme, Ezra Pound, T. S. Eliot, and others took the lead
in exploring, with a bold certainty of taste, the entire
literary horizon. In America, beginning in the twenties, the
New Critical activity centered around a group of Southern
writers, one of whom was Ransom himself; chief among
the others were Allen Tate, Robert Penn Warren, and
Cleanth Brooks. Although numerous other critics wrote
brilliant individual works that make up part of the canon
of the New Criticism, it was in these two groups of writers
that the fresh and novel ideas of the new approach made
something like a complete view of the world. Both groups

held that poems, in being complete and self-contained units of meaning, can be understood on their own terms, without dependence to historical or biographical material for explanation. But both groups, being strongly tradition-alist in outlook (though they were experimental in formal and technical matters), extended their literary canons to include general social and political concerns and thus incurred distaste and suspicion from the predominantly humanistic and liberal-minded literary establishment.

Whatever its political implications, however, the New Criticism was more than a revolt against liberalism and romanticism; it was a new way of regarding poetic knowledge — a way that has proved to be viable and rewarding. Occurring within one generation of literary critics, it has been carried on by their pupils; and, far from exhausting itself, has been largely absorbed into the entire literary profession, effecting considerable changes in the way literature is approached both inside and outside the academy. When one views the movement now, with some perspective in time, it is not difficult to discern that it arose as a rediscovery and a defense of the validity of imaginative truth. Ray B. West has written

> Those critics most commonly identified as the "new critics". . . . insist that they are not presenting a new view of literature, but are regaining an old view, lost or obscured by the temper of our age and the demands of an outworn, pseudoscientific scholarship. (*Essays in Modern Critical Theory*, pp. 116-117)

It is probably more accurate to say that the literary men participating in this movement were defending an old view of literature and of man with a criticism that was radically new — a criticism that, in complexity, subtlety, and the ability to make fundamental discriminations, was unlike any that had gone before.

The movement embraced men of diverse persuasion, as easily accommodating a liberal humanist as a high-church Anglican. Actually, however, though wide differences of conviction mark most of its practitioners, the New Critical movement may now be seen as the rather well-defined expression of a dominant tendency in literary thought during the first half of the twentieth century. (The Russian "formalist" school was developing its own similar principles during this same time, independent of the other two movements in England and America.) Though the new outlook was diffused among various sorts of persons, a generally applicable list of its distinguishing features can be assembled. One of its most important principles concerns the impersonality, or anonymity, of the poet as author of the poem; he is to be viewed as creative agency but not "owner" or even necessarily "knower" of his own work. Another chief credo of the movement is the assumption that the totality of the poem, what psychologists call the *gesalt,* contains its meaning, which is not to be found in any of its separable parts. Further, the New Criticism espouses an organic rather than a decorative view of metaphor and symbol, recognizing in these devices expressions of the non-rational element in man's mind — his *felt* as well as his *thought* life. A consequence of this tenet is the rejection of the dichotomy between form and content and the assignation of primacy to the imagination rather than the reason as the originating source of the poem. Finally, the New Criticism stresses the importance of the concrete in poetry, a body of details or a cluster of images that create a dense fabric of sense particulars expressive of feeling. A rich complication of language, employing irony, wit, paradox, ambiguity, and tension is thus a basic requirement for poetry, and close analysis of technique becomes the chief critical procedure.

This new attitude toward poetry has by now largely been absorbed into the entire profession of letters and, in some quarters, has itself become an oppressive orthodoxy. What its vital spirit has accomplished, however, is to solidify a body of principle as a base upon which systematic literary study may proceed. Indeed, since the fifties, various post-formalist movements have made themselves felt in literary criticism, all of them assisted, to a varying degree, by the seriousness and clarity with which the so-called New Critics regarded the problems of form and technique.

But though the various writers practicing the new method agreed on the appropriate strategy for understanding poetry, they did not agree on certain metaphysical or ethical extensions of poetic knowledge. The great dividing point among them occurred over the question of meaning. Does the poem (or drama or novel) make some sort of comment about reality? Or does it simply make pseudo-statements, in order to organize experience or to heighten and structure consciousness? Does it discover value already present in existence — or does it create a new realm of being? T. S. Eliot and the Southern critics — holding to a Christian world view — have been consistent in maintaining that the literary work is an analogue of an "order in reality." Only the Southerners however have gone on to develop an extensive criticism of literature based upon a complete metaphysical and cultural philosophy.

These Southern writers, who published the little magazine *The Fugitive* during the early 1920's, have held a unique place in modern criticism. Working on all fronts in the profession of letters — poetry, criticism, fiction, scholarship, biography, history, editorship, reviews, textbooks, pedagogy — they have had their greatest effect as a school in criticism. Directly, they gave to American letters its most important body of literary theory; indirectly, they engendered an enormously diversified and technically brilliant flow of literary explication from successive generations of students and associates. Their achievement has been to inaugurate in the modern world a true discipline of literary study given its proper position in relation to other bodies of thought.

John Crowe Ransom, Allen Tate, and Donald Davidson were the leaders of the twenty-five or so Fugitives and Agrarians; Robert Penn Warren, Cleanth Brooks, and Andrew Lytle were members of both companies or closely enough associated to be considered members. These men have produced their mature criticism largely apart from each other and have worked steadily in quite dissimilar veins; yet their writings make up a unified body of literary criticism in being the fruits of a fundamentally congruent view of the world — of what Allen Tate has called "a common historical myth."

IT WAS A MYTH first given form by family and community customs and early surroundings — they all grew up in the bluegrass region of Tennessee and Kentucky

— and fixed in their minds and imaginations by preparatory-school education in the classics and university study in the liberal arts. Thus these Southern poet-critics were shaped in sensibility and outlook by a society that, remarkably enough in the twentieth century, could still provide an experience of tradition and community. The region in which they spent their formative years held tenaciously to a heritage surviving from the classical-medieval synthesis, though certainly at times distorted and incomplete. For all its apparent provinciality the South was able to provide its young with a fund of ideas and feelings reaching back to antiquity. Still to be encountered in Southern society, for instance, was a sense of cosmic order, at a time when most of the rest of the Western world was caught in a growing sense of disorder and alienation. This essentially Hellenic trait was modified by a Biblical awareness of sin and accountability, tempered by a belief in "saving grace." Additionally, various relics of decorum shaped the conscience of the young person growing up in one of the few remaining places where memory and proper behavior still mattered: the chivalric virtues of loyalty and courtesy and a hierarchical social code shaped a demeanor ranging from stoic self-denial to bountiful generosity. Finally, surviving among the folk in particular was an oral tradition vital enough to preserve ballads and tales from the old days in a richly varied spoken language, at once metaphorical and plain, ironic and melancholy. All this is to say of course that, judged by the modern temper, the South that nurtured these men was more backward technologically and more illiterate than other parts of the country, more conservative in its beliefs, more poetic in its myths.

To regard THE FUGITIVE-AGRARIANS unequivocal-
ly, then, as New Critics — as pure Formalists, that is, in the
sense of being aestheticists who divorce the literary
document from any sort of social context — is to be mis-
led. For though they emphasize the integrity and objectivity of poetry and the special kind of knowledge which it
conveys, and though they decry a current tendency to
reduce poems to data serving other modes of cognition,
they have nonetheless testified over the years to the
existence of the poem in a total metaphysical and social
(political, if you will) order outside itself. Indeed, their
effort has been to renew the vitality of an art that has
become too bookish in its separation from life — to restore
its proper role in the continuum of human culture.

A further bond between the Southern critics — and in
many ways the most profound influence in their lives —
was their commitment to poetry in the association which
they formed as young college men, making up a community
of kindred spirits willing to submit their opinions and beliefs
to the "trial by poetry." The final shaping force in their
view of the world was their participation in Agrarianism in
the thirties, a consciously intellectual movement growing
out of an intense apprenticeship to the profession of
letters in the Fugitive activity of the twenties.

Their group had begun its formation at Vanderbilt
University in 1915 and 1916; but it was not until after the
War, when John Crowe Ransom and Donald Davidson
returned from overseas, that their meetings with the
others took a literary direction. It was not until this time,
too, in the early twenties, that Allen Tate had joined the

company, along with, somewhat later, Robert Penn Warren, and, unofficially, Cleanth Brooks and Andrew Lytle. Excitement was in the air; revolution of some sort seemed imminent; poetry was quite obviously to be its instrument. It is a familiar story; one encounters it from time to time among literati since the French Revolution: the literary circle, meeting at first for "creative" endeavor and mutual admiration and turning rather quickly to political and revolutionary concerns — except that, for the Fugitives, the revolutionary impulse and the iconoclasm remained literary and cultural and were to take the direction of restoring a tradition rather than destroying it. They met for a year or two before deciding to dare the launching of a publication; but once they had begun it, *The Fugitive* was to last four years (from April, 1922, to December, 1925) — a fairly long life in those days of emerging little magazines — and served to commit its editors to poetry and initiate them in their responsibilities as critics. Moreover, it was to make possible for them the astonishing revelation that as Southerners they possessed decided advantages, both as poets and critics. They found that they still held, instinctively, without effort, the "world picture" that Shakespeare had held; they understood from within, as they discovered, those pieties which undergird the entire Western literary tradition and which William Faulkner later came to call the "old verities." In this process of self-discovery, the Fugitives learned that they were gentlemen, Christians, and — if the egalitarian world forced them into admitting it — clearly aristocratic, at least in their attitude toward literature, education, and culture. And yet, a group of unabashed intellectuals, they found themselves increasingly on the

side of the folk rather than the academicians. Primarily for
this reason, they felt compelled to explore the relation of
the economic to the aesthetic life of a culture and to
examine the rival claims made by a humanistic secularism
and a traditional faith: in short, they moved on to their
"Agrarian" stage, wherein they frankly admitted the bonds
between literature and the rest of society. This direction in
their thought began among them soon after the suspension
of *The Fugitive* and was in fact an outgrowth of their
primary engagement with poetry and literary criticism.
Tate had moved to Tennessee after a sojourn in Paris and
New York and was studying Southern history, in
preparation for his biographies of Jefferson Davis (1928)
and Stonewall Jackson (1929). Warren and Brooks were
doing graduate study at Oxford; and Ransom and
Davidson were teaching at Vanderbilt and continuing their
writing. Davidson was editing the book page of the
Nashville *Tennessean*, reading hundreds of current books,
farming out reviews to his friends but doing most of them
himself. Ransom was occupied with his philosophic and
theological speculations, devoting himself to a manuscript
that he intended to call "Giants for Gods." (It appeared in
1930 as *God Without Thunder*.) Andrew Lytle had
returned to the South from New York and was at work on
his biography of Nathan Bedford Forrest (1931). All were
writing poetry. At about the same time, they began to see
in the Southern mode of life an instance of something very
valuable for the poet and, indeed, for the human race. For
Ransom the South was a region still holding to what he
called the "old religion" − which, based on a belief in the
stern and inscrutable God of Israel, still had a place in it
for myth, for piety toward nature, and for the

supernaturalism required by poetry. (*God Without Thunder*, p. 5) Tate saw it as a final instance of Western Christian humanism; in his biography of Jefferson Davis, he commented:

> The South was the last stronghold of European civilization in the Western hemisphere, a conservative check upon the restless expansiveness of the industrial North . . . permanently old-fashioned, backward-looking, slow, contented to live upon a modest conquest of nature, unwilling to conquer the earth's resources for the fun of conquest; contented, in short, to take only what man needs: unwilling to juggle the needs of man in the illusory pursuit of abstract wealth. (p. 301)

Donald Davidson's memoir of the movement (*Southern Writers in the Modern World*, 1957) described it as a conflict with far broader implications than the merely sectional. Speaking retrospectively of the Agrarian defense of "the cause of civilized society . . . against the new barbarism of science and technology controlled and directed by the modern power state," Davidson commented:

> Our quarrel was not with industry or science in their proper role, but with industrialism as a tyrant enslaving and ruling science itself, and with it religion, the arts, education, the state, thus reducing all principles to one principle, the economic, and becoming a destroyer, ready to break the continuity of human history and threatening the very existence of human society. (p. 57)

Andrew Lytle has since commented about the Agrarians (*Shenandoah,* Summer 1955):

They did not pretend to be other than amateurs in economics and history and theology. But being trained in the word, they might write more convincingly than specialists. They might and did relate economics through history to the immediate situation, as specialists cannot do. This led them at least to see that the local malaise was not endemic but epidemic. The local scene was brought not only into new relationship with this country or Europe but within that of Christian civilization. This perhaps can be called the Southern attitude as distinct from that of the rest of American letters. (p. 33)

The first action of the Agrarians as a group was the publication of a collection of essays entitled, after much argument, *I'll Take My Stand* (1930). A general manifesto, headed "A Statement of Principles," written by Ransom but endorsed by the others, served as an introduction to the volume and made clear the dimensions of the attack. In it industrialism is defined as "the economic organization of the collective American society," and its cause named as "the decision of society to invest its economic resources in the applied sciences." In an industrial society, the essay contends, "religion can hardly be expected to flourish," since it derives from "a submission to the general intention of a nature that is fairly inscrutable." (p. xxiv)   Nor, it continues, can the arts and the amenities of life, both dependent on a wholeness of sensibility, long survive the onslaughts of technology.

Eight of the twelve essays in the volume were written by literary men, most of them connected at one time or another with the Vanderbilt Department of English and hence under the direct influence of the "Fugitive" spirit: the number included — besides Ransom, Tate, Davidson,

Warren, and Lytle — John Donald Wade, graduate of the University of Georgia, Harvard, and Columbia, then teaching on the English staff at Vanderbilt; Stark Young, the New York drama critic from Mississippi; and John Gould Fletcher, expatriate Arkansas poet then living in England. It was an impressive gathering of humanely educated men who dared to speak on matters outside their specialties. They were not well received.

When one rereads the Agrarian symposium in the light of subsequent events it is clear that the object of attack was secularism with its redefinition of man, rather than mere technology. What was being defended, likewise, rather than agrarianism *per se* was the traditional image of man as repository of the pieties that gave rise to the Western communal virtues, still available, to some degree at least, in the South. As Donald Davidson has described the "total purpose" of the movement, it was

> to seek the image of the South which we could cherish with high conviction and to give it, wherever we could, the finality of art in those forms, fictional, poetical, or dramatic, that have the character of myth and therefore, resting on belief, secure belief in others and, unlike arguments, are unanswerable, are in themselves fulfilled and complete. Such was the total purpose, of which the so-called Agrarian movement was but a declaratory preface." (*Southern Writers in the Modern World*. p. 60)

Practically speaking, of course, one must say that the Agrarian movement failed — in the South as elsewhere. It failed to stop the tide of urbanization or the technological revolution; it failed to rally Southerners or other sympathizers to any kind of mobilization against a menacing technocracy. Though a second collection of essays appeared in 1936 (*Who Owns America?*, edited by Herbert Agar and Allen Tate), by the beginning of the forties the Agrarians themselves began to realize the impracticability of any direct resistance against scientific and technological progress. Ransom announced his departure from an Agrarian position in 1940; Tate had never fully embraced the program as an ultimate commitment, regarding the South always in its larger context of Christendom. Warren, not greatly involved in the movement, turned his chief energies to his novels and to a troubled concern for the American Negro. Brooks, though sympathetic, had not made the cause directly his own. Only Donald Davidson and Andrew Lytle held to the Agrarian aims, refusing to leave the South, either physically or spiritually.

During the thirties, however, RANSOM, TATE, and DAVIDSON devoted their major efforts to the reforming of culture through criticism; and in no sense did the Agrarian "incarnation" of the Fugitive group represent a mere side issue. They published dozens of articles in national journals during this time – chiefly in the new *American Review* (1933-37). Everything they wrote in this period of productivity contributed to their central positions; none of it was simply a "phase" of their development. Though Ransom turned away from Agrarianism as a movement, he never really changed his views, nor did Tate basically modify his outlook. Davidson, of course, continued the battle overtly to the end of his life. (He died in April 1968.) Tate and Ransom both went on to interests that for each held a higher value.

Ransom took on the editorship of the *Kenyon Review* and gave body to his literary speculations under the guidance of Kantian philosophy. Tate continued his intense work as a poet and critic, editing the *Sewanee Review* for two years and remodeling it completely; but finally his essentially religious examination of culture led him to Catholicism and to a less desperate intellectual position. At the time, however, Ransom, Tate, and Davidson produced analyses of cultural crisis as cogent as the world is likely to know. Despite the apparent futility of the agrarian effort at the time, one must recognize that a great part of "post-modern" thought has stemmed from the principles developed in Agrarian criticism, which rested in large part on the foundation of Fugitive poetry.

These three, Ransom, Tate, and Davidson, were the originators of a distinct body of criticism, making of that activity a discipline for which in our time there is no adequate designation. Refusing to limit themselves to explication, analysis, or theory, their task became nothing short of the reunion of fragmented man, so that thought and feeling, imagination and memory, piety and creativity could coexist once more in the human frame. They developed their world picture, or paradigm, from a faithful attention to the poetic act, finding in it the proper norms for human action, given form by the entire course of Western Civilization, incarnate for the last time, as it seemed, in the South. Each found his own perspective for viewing that cultural order as well as his own relation to it. Out of this perspective, for each, came a complete poetics, a structure of literary values viewed from a specific vantage point.

In his preface to *The Man of Letters in the Modern*

World Tate makes a comment illuminating to his own criticism, as well as to Ransom's and Davidson's. He speaks of the "gradual discovery of potentialities of the mind that must always have been there," and goes on to remark the "point of view" by which the literary critic is "governed." The importance of point of view, he observes, lies in what one can *see* by means of it. "Of the range and direction of a point of view, and why a point of view exists in some persons, nobody can be certain." However learned a critic might be as a person, Tate makes clear, as a critic he knows virtually nothing; his importance lies in what he sees.

It is precisely this characteristic that is most remarkable in these three Fugitive poet-critics: their absolute fidelity to point of view. They are not simply men of erudition and wisdom writing about ideas in superbly articulated rhetoric. They are this, but more: they are men guided by well defined perspectives; and both their poetry and criticism bear witness to the integrity and uniqueness of their vision.

What they see is focused upon the symbol of the land. It is for them that body of the world which brings into concentration the entire meaning of life. Primarily the land, as symbol, is the good society; but it carries within itself by a complex set of analogies all human values. The South first made the Fugitive-Agrarians aware of their subject, though the South has not really been that subject. Rather, they found in the defeat of the South an instance of the loss of the land; further, they were made aware of the universal plight of modern man and his homelessness by the threat of industrialism to a beloved region. But, just as Dante's central reality is a woman, and Virgil's is a city, for these three, the land itself — and man's relation to it —

is the poignant reality to which their souls resonated, in their criticism as well as their poetry.

If they share a central symbol — the land — they view it from different angles. Davidson's view is lyric and heroic; his normal attitude is that of consummation or of epic striving to regain the homeland. His attacks and denunciations stem from a fierce, almost feral defensiveness for his tribal community. The archetypal vision which recurs to him again and again is one of possession of the land; his is the pastoral voice celebrating the songs of youth and love, the virtues of faith and loyalty.

In contrast Tate's view is tragic. It is the anguish of the loss of the land that has tormented him throughout his literary career. The loss reaches back, past the seventeenth century into antiquity, past the fall of Troy to the archetypal loss of the garden. Like Hamlet, Tate ruminates on the meaning of life and death; like Tiresias he foresees the encroaching darkness; like the preacher in *Ecclesiastes* he is preoccupied with the vanity of earthly wishes. His chief themes are sin and salvation; he castigates society, like a prophet. His eye is filled always with the tragic vision of the impossibility of human achievement.

Ransom's angle of vision is essentially comic. Rueful, wry, ironic, he "endures," and, even more, accepts. The land which he loves has been so long in disorder that the right hierarchy can hardly be hoped for; it must be celebrated by the remnant in little "pockets of culture" (a phrase he used in an address at Vanderbilt in 1951). Good manners, courtesy, rituals are all important because man is cut off from the garden and must make his way in a world of desperate difficulties. But there is sentiment and devotion, and the world's body is inexhaustibly interesting.

The consistency of these critics comes not from the simple logic of their statements, but from their correspondence to a coherent image of life, depicted from a post of observation explored first in poetic and only subsequently in rhetorical form. Their uniqueness lies in the fact that they demonstrate in their criticism fully as much as in their poetry the authenticity and objectivity provided by the creative imagination. Their critical vision is an extension of the structure of the poetic insight. They are true to what they see and, consequently, their criticism is really as "anonymous" as their poems. What they provide, then, is a universal set of standards for the right order of human behavior: a vision of the good society lies behind the filters of their separate viewpoints.

JOHN CROWE RANSOM, Rhodes Scholar and son of a Tennessee Methodist minister, was the dean of the Fugitives — presiding genius at meetings and standard-bearer of critical judgment. Born into a learned family in Pulaski, Tennessee, April 30, 1888, he was given an excellent classical education before he entered Vanderbilt in 1903. He returned to Vanderbilt to teach in 1914, after a three-year stay at Oxford, where he had spent most of his time reading in philosophy. Turning away from the abstraction of philosophic studies, however, he discovered something which he must have known before his graduate education — the complicated richness of the "world's body" as it was revealed in poetry. It was

Ransom who interested the other Fugitives (his pupils and colleagues) in trying their hands at poetic composition; they had all had the benefit of literary educations, of course, and felt perfectly at home with classical and English literature, without extending their interest to contemporary poetry. With the publication of Ransom's volume *Poems about God* (1919), however, conversation at Saturday-night sessions began to center on the new poetry and literary questions in general. Ransom criticized the other Fugitives' first efforts, in a genial and courteous, though unsparing, manner. He would read a text closely, line by line, giving close attention to its verbal ambiguities and details of meter, rhyme, and syntax. This method came to be the practice at Fugitive gatherings, with heated argument many times resulting from the stubborn defense of conflicting aesthetic and linguistic convictions. Something of Ransom's formal style was adopted by the entire group, as were many of his critical ideas.

One of Ransom's strongest aesthetic presuppositions made its appearance in these early sessions: that poetry is born of experience, not of innocence; it is "post-scientific," rather than "pre-scientific," as he later expresses it — not the work of a child or of "that eternal youth that is in some women," (p. viii) but of a sensible and masculine adult. For, though poetry honors the feminine — the realm of feeling and value — it is not the expression of the feminine or of the childish. It is not written by sentimentalists or innocents or holy fools, but by those who have struggled with the world. Ransom was not to make this position explicit until the late thirties, with the publication of *The World's Body*; but it is this attitude that has governed his own work all along, his poetry as well as his prose.

A second principle controlling his total vision has caused him to be called a "dualist": this is the tenet that in a poem the prose meaning, a logical "structure," as he was later to call it, is made to submit to an apparently unrelated and independent body of sense particulars of both sound and imagery, the "texture" of the poem, in what he sometimes calls a "miracle" of equilibrium. All his other generative ideas — those concerning myth, form, "metaphysical poetry," and the anonymity of the poet — are related to this structure-texture reconciliation, a theme to which he has returned again and again throughout his entire career. His position on this question, however, does not in reality constitute a dualism so much as a dynamism; he is concerned with a total pattern of poetic action, the imaginative process. But however one wishes to categorize his position, what must be seen as underlying all Ransom's critical thought is the conviction that a complete act of knowledge consists, first, of the formation, by abstraction, of some general notion of how things ought to be and then, later, the discovery, in an encounter with the actual world, that things are not after all quite so simple. It is this submission to the reality outside the mind without any relinquishment of the governing idea within the mind that, according to Ransom, has created myth, culture, tradition, manners, and poems.

Certainly Ransom's was the most original critical mind in the Fugitive group, though each of the other important poet-critics — Tate, Davidson, Warren, Brooks, and Lytle — was to extend his ideas further and perhaps provide the definitive development of something Ransom had merely indicated. Each of the others had his own originality, his own insight; but the total structure which each made rested on a foundation that John Ransom helped build. Perhaps this is only to say that he was their teacher.

Even in his first critical pieces, the early essays in *The Fugitive*, as well as in his letters to absent members of the group, one detects the keenly theoretical intelligence at work; and the permanent themes are already present. In the first editorial essay in the magazine, "The Future of Poetry," (February 1924) he advances one of the ideas that was to hold constant interest for him:

> it does not seem too hazardous to claim that poetry, as one of the formal arts, has for its specific problem to play a dual role with words; to conduct a logical sequence with their meanings on the one hand; and to realize an objective pattern with their sounds on the other. Now between the meanings of words and their sounds there is ordinarily no discoverable relation except one of accident; and it is therefore miraculous, to the mystic, when words which make sense can also make a uniform objective structure of accents and rhymes. It is a miracle of harmony, of the adaptation of the free inner life to the outward necessity of things. (p. 142)

This sense of a "miracle" in poetry's reconciliation of unrelated interests remains a cornerstone in Ransom's aesthetic position and finds recurrent expression in his writings, poetic and critical.

Another essay in *The Fugitive,* "Thoughts on the Poetic Discontent," in the June 1925 issue, brings up an equally important topic for his canon: "Irony," he writes, "may be regarded as the ultimate mode of the great minds − it presupposes the others." To explain the origins of irony, Ransom constructs a little myth: Man finds a chasm between himself and the objective world, and so tends in his youth to "effect an escape from dualism" by constructing an illusion of "mystical community" in which he participates with nature. But his romantic escape cannot prevail in view of the facts of experience; consequently man is obliged to accept a dualism once more – this time, however, a seasoned dualism; and his rejection of the romantic illusion is so "unwilling," with so much "music and color and romantic mystery" remaining, that its fruit is irony and poetry rather than despair and cynicism. Irony is thus a transcendent attitude, the position of equilibrium, attained by man as his ideal construct is modified by the experience of fallen nature. It is "the rarest of the states of mind," Ransom observes, "because it is the most inclusive; the whole mind has been active in arriving at it, both creation and criticism, both poetry and science." From the vantage point of irony, then, the complexities in man's experience of the world can be reconciled. Not only Ransom's later criticism, but the writing of all the Fugitive critics – with the possible exception of Davidson – was to be based on this attitude of inclusion, first stated here.

Ransom worked out in 1926 a complete theory of the aesthetic process in a study he never published, a book-length manuscript entitled "The Third Moment" – a "kind of Prolegomena to Any Future Poetic," as he wrote Tate. (Sept. 5, 1926) Apparently the work was rejected by a publishing company and Ransom "consigned it to flames." Records of its chief concerns remain in Ransom's correspondence with Tate, however, and one can see that this formulation of his theories was important to Ransom's critical thought during the rest of his career. He traced in his manuscript the three moments "in the historical order of Experience." The first moment is the original experience of life — intense, unfallen, complete: "Pure of all intellectual content, unreflective, concrete, and singular . . . " The second moment manifests itself as a period of thought, of analysis, of recording experience; it proceeds by the formation of concepts through an abstraction from the total experience. The third moment begins with memory and a sense of loss: "we become aware of the deficiency of the record . . . All our concepts and all our histories put together cannot add up into the wholeness with which we start out."

The fullness of the first moment can be recaptured only by the creative act, the making of images. "The Imagination is the faculty of Pure Memory, or unconscious mind; it brings out the original experiences from the dark storeroom, where we dwell upon them with a joy proportionate to our previous despair . . ." We construct dreams, fancies, morals, art, religion — all images made in an attempt to recapture the "fugitive first moment." The result of this construction of images is a "mixed world" in which images coexist with previously formed concepts. Poetry presents this mixed world in its complexity, exhibiting always the opposition and then the reconciliation "between the Conceptual or Formal and the Individual or Concrete." The opposition displays itself most acutely and tragically in poetry "when the concepts referred back to reality are the dearest concepts."

Another large-scale work written fairly early in Ransom's career is scarcely better known than his unpublished volume. *God Without Thunder* (1930), issuing from the press in the same year as the Agrarian volume (*I'll Take My Stand*), is a work central to the understanding of Agrarianism, as well as the whole body of Fugitive-Agrarian criticism. It is surprising that the remarkable originality of this book has been so little noted; ideas throughout its pages anticipate Carl Jung, Mircea Eliade, Eric Voegelin, Susanne Langer, Philip Wheelwright, and other critics treating the topics of myth, symbol, and culture. But though Ransom's understanding of these matters is quite modern, his total vision is based very firmly on early Protestant Orthodoxy (the religious terminology provides the book with its richly wry and ironic tone). *God Without Thunder* is not about religion, however, despite its open references to it; it is about myth and culture and the way in which human beings transform abstract notions through their love of sensible objects. It is also about a tendency of society to destroy itself through what Ransom chooses to call "science" − actually a death drive that has the appearance of a life force. The fall of man came about, he maintains, from the hybris of attempting to control nature through scientific knowledge, as the myths both of the Garden of Eden and of Prometheus testify.

And the decline continues. "Ours is a time," Ransom writes, "in which an old body of thought is being progressively disbelieved and a new body of thought is progressively governing our conduct." (p. 4) Because of our growing assurance of rational explanations for all phenomena, "Orthodox Christianity," based on a belief in "the stern and inscrutable God of Israel, the God of the Old Testament," (p. 5) is increasingly being discarded for a secular "religious" dogma, an aberration of the Christian teaching. This diluted religion posits an amiable and understandable God who is the embodiment of general benevolence and social welfare. He is a God without Thunder, demanding nothing extraordinary or supernatural.

At the same time, industrialism is surrounding modern man with an artificial environment which destroys his sense of contingency and gives him the illusion of absolute control over nature and himself. His hours of leisure are spent increasingly on trivia. Even his richly emotive symbolism associated with love is progressively degraded by rationalistic attitudes, so that scientific concern replaces the poetic and religious: "Love is the aesthetic and lust is the science of sex," (p. 141) Ransom maintains.

Ransom's prescription for the Western mind, caught in this dire predicament, is myth: "A myth," he tells us, "is a fable; it calmly alleges a miracle or impossible occurrence; . . . it leaves its natural history altogether and yet attempts to imply the whole of that history. Myth resorts to the supernatural in order to represent the fullness of the natural." But modern man will not consider the supernatural; consequently Ransom advocates defining myth for the secularist "in terms of its psychic necessity," as a symbolic projection of fundamental human feeling, rather than as theological or metaphysical reality. This would be, he writes, "a sort of natural history of supernaturalism," a method which he admits to be "a quite unorthodox way to justify orthodoxy," though he considers it the only remaining means available at present.

In his essay written for the Agrarian symposium, "Reconstructed but Unregenerate," Ransom continued his attack on the new religion. "The good life depends on leisure," he writes. And leisure can be obtained in a society only by "a prevailing magnanimity which scorns personal advancement at the expense of the free activity of the mind." (p. 10) "The two gospels of the modern world," however, according to Ransom, are Progress and Service, which will "lure" man into kindhearted activity in further and further attempts to overcome nature and thus prevent any leisure at all. (p. 11)

Ransom was later to turn his attention away from the cultural and religious concerns of *God Without Thunder* but he was never to desert the principles which they caused him to formulate. Indeed, most of his critical writing during the thirties stemmed directly from his Agrarian commitment. In *The World's Body* (1938), one of the most important landmarks in modern criticism, Ransom brought together fifteen essays on poetry and the specifically poetic mode of knowledge; but far from being purely exegetical in their concerns, these essays imply an entire universe delineated by his social and cultural thought. At least two of the pieces in *The World's Body* are classics; both convey so intimate and engaging a sense of the pleasures of poetry that they teach as much by personal witness as by the formulation of principles.

In one of them, "Forms and Citizens," Ransom is still concerned with poetry in its cultural context, defending ritual and custom in both manners and art. Denouncing the straightforward approach of the pragmatic mind toward its object, he declares that in such direct action the knower totally devours his object, having made it of no worth beyond that of self-gratification. The indirect approach through ritual, he asserts, not only restrains the predatory tendencies of the seeker: it actually augments the worth of the thing or person sought after. After discussing the value of form as a mode of indirection in lovemaking and in the confrontation of death (producing courtship and funeral rituals), Ransom goes on by analogy to justify formal versification in poetry. The poetic imagination is a model of indirection par excellence, he points out; formally restraining itself from immediate possession, its aim is to enhance the value of the object through close and reverent attention.

This enunciation of an epistemology of poetic knowledge is followed by an essay on the nature of poetry: "Poetry: A Note in Ontology" is the *locus classicus* for Ransom's elaboration upon the dualistic tension inside the poetic act. In this essay he differentiates between Physical poetry, which is about things, and Platonic poetry, which is about ideas. To render its objects, Physical poetry employs images, these possessing, as he says, "a primordial freshness which idea can never claim." (p. 115) Continuing his disparagement of ideational poetry, Ransom writes, "An idea is derivative and tamed," whereas "the image is in the natural or wild state, and it has to be discovered there, not put there, obeying its own law and none of ours." The "fine Platonic world of ideas" does not match the "original world of perception . . . populated by the stubborn and contingent objects. . . ." (p.123) It is in our memory, he tells us, that we find images still full and complete, not paled by abstraction or distorted into simplistic "values" by practical men. But poetry cannot exist as pure wildness or "thinginess"; it must submit to the disciplined control of logic and meter. In fact, Ransom makes clear his doubt of the reputed innocence of the "aesthetic moment" which

Schopenhauer praised. Instead, he asserts the complexity of poetic cognition:

> The aesthetic moment appears as a curious moment of suspension; between the Platonism in us, which is militant, always sciencing and devouring, and a starved inhibited aspiration towards innocence which, if it could only be free, would like to respect and know the object as it might of its own accord reveal itself. (p.130)

The poetry that best records this suspended moment is metaphysical poetry--the poetry that deals with things but introduces the "miracle": a figure that deserts the credible surface of life to express the fullest possible reality in life. It employs a miraculism that "arises when the poet discovers by analogy an identity between objects which is partial, though it should be considerable, and proceeds to an identification which is complete." (p.139)

After *The World's Body*, Ransom's critical principles are basically fixed; he may later alter his emphases here and there, or his own attitudes, but not his world view or his placement of poetry within that world. In his next volume, *The New Criticism* (1941), he analyzes characteristics of what he terms a new sort of criticism, and though he never completely defines this innovative method, one can infer from his remarks throughout the book that it is not so much a single way of proceeding as a general recognition of the ontological status of the poem.

He examines the critical systems of I. A. Richards, T. S. Eliot, and Yvor Winters, concluding with a chapter of his own, entitled "Wanted: An Ontological Critic." In it he searches for the differentia of poetry--the specific attribute defining the poetic mode of discourse. A clue to this distinguishing feature is to be found in its "odd structure";

the poem is "a loose logical structure with an irrelevant local texture." Unlike other modes of discourse, the poem possesses a structure in which the rational thrust is modified and controlled by apparently extraneous matter. And its content can be of any sort. Obviously, then, for Ransom, it must be the *order* which is the differentiating principle of a poem, not the kind of content or the strictly logical sequence of thought. The "worlds" given us by our scientific discourses are "reduced, emasculated, and docile versions" of the world in which we live, Ransom goes on to say. "Poetry intends to recover the denser and more refractory original world which we know loosely through our perceptions and memories. By this supposition it is a kind of knowledge which is radically or ontologically distinct." (p. 281) Ransom finds in his earlier-stated re-conciliation theory a key to the ontology of the poem. It is in counterpointing the meter with the meaning, two interests that are basically unlike, that the poet begins to bring "into experience both a denser and a more contingent world" and to command "a discourse in more dimensions." (p. 330) This peculiarly poetic kind of order is to be created by an ontological "law": "The two properties [that are united] shall not be identical, or like, or homogeneous, they shall be other, unlike, and hetero-geneous. It is the law of the actual world everywhere." (p. 327)

A decade later, in "Why Critics Don't Go Mad" (1952) Ransom speaks again of the two forces contending with each other within the poem, referring to his statement in *The New Criticism*:

> I had the idea of a poem as a great "paradox," a construct looking two ways, with logic trying to

> dominate the metaphors and metaphors trying to
> dominate the logic. . . but we must reckon with the
> meters too, and the poem assumes the form of a
> trinitarian existence. (Poems and Essays, p. 151)

And in another essay written that same year reviewing the
Chicago critics ("Humanism at Chicago"), Ransom gives
further attention to this "trinitarian" scheme, suggesting
that we consider a poem as realizing not simply one object,
but "three objects at once." But in this description the
clearly drawn oppositions of logic and metaphor begin to
blur. Ransom mentions the logical construct first, as
holding the "primary interest" of the poet. He calls it
"plot" or, more inclusively, "argument," and instead of
remaining derivative and tamed in the realm of pure logic,
it has already blended in with "the world of affairs"–it is
'ethical," "social," "useful."

The second object develops "irresistibly" out of many
lesser concerns into "a small version of our natural world
in its original dignity." The vision which the poet
encounters here is Edenic, not Platonic. In this scheme the
first object retains the function of uninterfered logicality,
and the second of concretion. But the awareness of the
fallen world has now advanced from second position, its
place in earlier models, into the first, and the second
object becomes the proper residence of the unfallen state:

> And now, within the same poem, we can pass
> from one world to another. The first world is the
> hustling one we have to live in, and we want it to
> be as handsome as possible. The second world is
> the one we think we remember to have come from,
> and we will not let it go.
> There is but one big construct left in the poem:
> the metered one. . .The rhythm of the meters

envelops the two other objects, like an atmosphere;
it is a constraint and a blessing too. For it is
sounding all the time; it is a low-grade music
making an elemental, comic, and eternal object.
Very diffidently I venture to construe it. I think
the meters are an apt imitation of the Platonic
Ideas. . .For the worst thing about those two
worlds is that the objects and arrangements we
sense so exquisitely and cherish so deeply are
doomed; they are mortal. That awareness is never
withheld from us in the poem, but quite the
contrary. Nor is there any human equivalent for
them, really, in a world of Platonic Ideas. . . But
still the world has the distinction of being the
world of the immortals, and we like to sense it
presiding over us. (*Poems and Essays,* pp. 99-101)

Ransom now sees the poem as its creator would see it,
rather than as it would present itself to the
critic-philosopher. For the latter always keeps before him
the vision of the way things ought to be, but the poet--and
here Ransom profits from the knowledge culled from his
own craft — sees first the "world of affairs" and then goes
back to remember the better world. Although he still sees
the poem as one moment containing three more or less
distinct objects, in this passage Ransom concerns himself
with the psychic origin of the poem, thereby allowing a
separation in ontological time of the three objects. A year
later, in his article on Blackmur ("More Than Gesture")
Ransom refines the idea further:

A powerful sensibility is recording in the poem,
and the result might be a tropical wilderness of
dense figurations, therefore humanly a waste, a

> nothing, but an equally powerful scheme of order
> is working there too, to shape and manage the
> riches of sense. The poem is conceived under the
> familiar figure of sensibility and intelligence acting
> in opposed parts and continually interacting; like
> parties in a drama or a dance; like a musical
> counterpoint. (*Poems and Essays,* p. 103)

The dualism of sensibilia and intellect is working out
its balance in a poem, he maintains, and more than that,
working it out beautifully, so that nothing is lost from
either side in the process. "But there is more," Ransom
continues;

> ... another interaction, involving a third part in the
> poem. It is the meter, and the musical phrasing.
> Here the relation is between the prose rhythms of
> the language and the imposed meters, and that
> opposition is fruitful too. The resultant language
> has an access of authority which is almost
> miraculous. (pp. 103-4)

Commenting on these statements some thirteen years
afterwards ("Theory of Poetic Form," *Texas Quarterly,*
Spring 1966) he writes, "Once in an essay I tried by a
figure of speech to explain the intricacy of the
arrangement. I spoke of the possibility of a structure
having a texture which is not quite in harmony with it."
(p. 198) He would prefer another figure now, he
maintains. He would speak of a poem "as assembling a
small universe of objects and actions, in which a thing, in
order to exist, must coexist with many other things which
are quite unlike it; and very comfortably, as the real world
demonstrates." (p. 199)

What Ransom has discerned in the world — and found
reflected in poetry — is a peculiar harmony, a
"miraculous" blending of disparates into an ordered

whole. He has declared in one of his most recent essays that he has never departed from the religion learned from his father at the turn of the century. And it is true that, for all his philosophical preoccupations, his view of the world is essentially religious and theistic; he has experienced it in the mode of the Biblical faith. His intellect was formed by the classics and matured by the moderns; Kant, Hegel, Schopenhauer, and Bergson, among others, have vied with Plato and Aristotle in his thinking. Like these nineteenth-century philosophers, he is fundamentally anti-rationalistic, with a mistrust of scientific abstraction deriving not so much from their influence as from an inherently poetic mode of thought. Still, for all his anti-abstractionism, Ransom has never been able to relinquish in his poetic theory the emphasis on logical meaning. Poetic knowledge is, for him, not unrelated to life in general. He rebukes Cleanth Brooks for objecting to the paraphrase of a poem and quarrels with Richard Blackmur for treating the ideas in a poetic structure as having no importance in the real world, even though they may be ideas upon which, at the very moment, out in the world of action, crucially important issues of life and death depend. "No faith, no passion of any kind," he tells us, "is originated in a poem; it is brought into the poem by the 'imitating' of life (to use Aristotle's term); it is the fact which is the heart of the fiction." (*Poems and Essays,* p. 107)

The poetic universe, then, to Ransom is a small, complex model which sets in motion and reconciles three modes of experience which have become, to civilized man, quite disparate and unrelated: first, rational experience; second, the experience of feeling and desire; third, the grand universals that cannot be stated, but only sounded — in a measured rhythm that calls all the language of the poem to an observance of its punctuation. The poem gives men knowledge that is applicable to the world of affairs; it reminds them of their myths; it teaches them restraint and piety.

ALLEN TATE'S essays are of an entirely different sort from Ransom's in purpose and occasion, as well as style and stance. Ransom, concerned with the poetic structure and process, is himself the ontological critic whom he ostensibly sought in *The New Criticism*. Tate's interest, in comparison, has always been essentially metaphysical and theological. A vision of the transcendent reality symbolized by literature has given lucidity to his analysis of form and control to his anatomy of culture.

Tate has assumed the role of protagonist for the literary mode of knowledge, a defender of the faith in a faithless age. Born in Winchester, Kentucky, on November 19, 1899, he had a haphazard but nonetheless classical education in Nashville, Louisville, Ashland, Evansville, and Washington, D.C., before entering Vanderbilt in 1918. In truth his principal early education, as with the other Fugitives, was gained at home, and his later postbaccalaureate education was chiefly under the tutelage of his own driving intellect. Upon graduating from Vanderbilt he undertook the rigorous, hazardous life of a man of letters with a zeal that did not admit of failure. Ransom teased him in the early days of his professional career, writing, "You get hold of a beautiful intuition and immediately antagonize your followers by founding a

Church thereon." Tate later apologized for the "toplofty tone" of some of his early essays; but despite this flaw – if indeed it is a flaw – from the beginning the essays indicate an incisive and original mind turned seriously toward the estate of letters. Tate developed his critical standards as a professional reviewer for the *Nation* and the *New Republic,* among other journals; consequently, he has indicated in his preface to the *Collected Essays,* the topics were chiefly those that happened to come to him as a reviewer, and the problem, as he puts it, was how much of his "imperfect insight and small knowledge" to draw upon in reviewing. On the contrary, one must protest, Tate's achievement is not only to have packed within the strictures of the literary review wide-ranging knowledge and insight, but also to have developed, in the course of diverse essays, a consistent critical outlook.

In Tate's first essays and letters he reveals the two conflicting impulses that were always to dominate his critical thought: his search for wholeness and harmony and his sense of fragmentation and loss. The first of these traits would cause him to seek for standards, for right principles embodied in specific works; the second would cause him to find these standards never quite available, to find man always an alien in the temporal world. To Davidson, loyal and devoted to his native region, Tate maintained that one cannot recapture the past, that neither the heroic mode nor the lyric voice can be used in times of disintegration, when a society has lost its coherence. To Ransom he maintained that the traditional body of literary techniques cannot be used by the modern poet; neither traditional meters, which Ransom valued so highly in his poetics, nor the ordinary poetic idiom could be used without radical dislocation. He differed strongly with Ransom on the entire question of the rational order controlling the poem, holding that modern poetry must include the complete range of consciousness. ("One Escape from the Dilemma," *The Fugitive,* April 1924) A year later he wrote Davidson about the inclusive nature of poetry:

> Poetry is to me successive instances of the whole rhythm of thought, and that includes reason, emotion, extralogical experience, or, as I put it a year or so ago, the entire phantasy of sensation. (July 25, 1925)

Tate's own poetry deserts the framework of narrative or logical sequence and displays supra-rational elements of suggestion and association. Its obliquities form strange and unexpected domains of meaning, rather than, like Ransom's, casting commonsense materials in a fresh light.

As modern and experimental in his own poetry as he was, Tate nonetheless directed his mind toward Orthodoxy of a stricter kind than Ransom's. In fact, he wrote Davidson from Paris as early as 1929 that he found himself more and more drawn to Catholicism – a good score of years before he did, in actuality, enter the Catholic Church. Tate's quest throughout all his writing was for the sacramental vision such as Dante's Christianity embodied; for the unity of being, achieved in the philosophy of Thomism; for the classical-Christian synthesis of thought and feeling, formed in the Middle Ages and still underlying, albeit fragmentarily, the Southern sensibility.

One of Tate's first published essays, "Poetry and the Absolute," (Sewanee Review, January 1927) is a protest against John Ransom's early dualistic thoery of poetic knowledge. Though Tate never reprinted this essay and apparently does not consider it part of his canon, it is never-

theless important to his total position. In his concern with
the epistemology of the poetic experience, Tate attempts
to distinguish "between a poetic absolute and the defined
absolute of systematic metaphysics." (p. 43) Both
philosophy and poetry, he proposes, are alike in personal
motivation; both come out of "the need of constructing a
'portrait of reality.'" In his attempt to describe the
"mimesis" of poetry, its mode of representing an
experience of the world, Tate in this essay gives explicit
allegiance to Aristotle's philosophical "realism" as
expressed in the *Metaphysics* and the *Poetics,* and strongly
rejects the strain of poetry-as-absolute developed in
German Idealism. The epistemology which he proposes,
though only roughly outlined, is indeed quite realistic in
its emphases. Language, he says, is the "signification" of a
"process" or cognitive act. (p. 44) And thus the poet in
dealing with language attempts to refine and intensify his
understanding of the experience contained in language
until he can "come to absolute terms" with a poetic
situation. A certain experience, then, receives an "absolute
quality," or completeness, through the poem. Tate
proposes that the end toward which poetry strives is "a
signification of experience that becomes absolute within
the dimensions of the poem." (p. 46) Thus the poet can
have an absolute knowledge as he gives form to his
experience, and the same absolute experience can be
grasped by the reader through the "perfectly realized
perceptions" which the poem contains.

Soon after the essay appeared, Ransom wrote Tate
rebuking him for an overemphasis on the "unqualified
Absolute" into which he makes the poetic experience, and
called him back to what he purported to see in Tate, his

own dualist equilibrium. But Tate's aesthetic was not to be
the same as Ransom's, though he had learned immensely
from him. He differed with Ransom, as did Aristotle with
his teacher Plato, and on much the same grounds. The
aesthetic expressed in "Poetry and the Absolute" was of
course to be more fully articulated and modified
considerably in Tate's later work. Nevertheless, in his
attempt to analyze the unique quality of good poetry, and
in his emphasis on the poet's role of giving individual form
to an experience of the common-sense world, Tate here
reveals some of the major aesthetic tendencies of his later
essays. He was not to understand completely his own
critical vision until he encountered Jacques Maritain and
undertook a serious study of Thomism. It is only in "The
Symbolic Imagination" (1951) and in papers following it
that Tate is able to deal fully with the metaphysical
implications of the poetic absolute.

The Agrarian enthusiasm which he shared with Ransom
and Davidson grew out of his study of Southern history
and his preoccupation with the role of science in a
traditional society. He wrote to Davidson at the time of
the Dayton trials " . . . I'm afraid I agree with Sanborn (his
philosophy teacher at Vanderbilt) that science has very
little to say for itself. I remember he used to emphasize
that view, but I scoffed at it: I see he was right." (March 3,
1926) Tate's biographies of Stonewall Jackson and of
Jefferson Davis turned his mind more directly to the
question of a traditional society and its effect on men's
characters. The American South, as a traditional society,
produced men of very nearly whole sensibilities; but this
society was being invaded by science, which, by its very
nature, is inimical to tradition and to the unity of life

engendered by traditional beliefs. It is not science as knowledge he opposes, Tate makes clear, but science as a mode of abstract thought dominating religion and discarding tradition. This outlook, which he calls positivism, is of course valid in science itself; but it can deliver only a partial view of reality, he maintains, the merely useful part. As Tate proposed in "Religion in the South," his essay in *I'll Take My Stand*, religion considers the "whole horse" and not just the working part, the horse power, the horse as machine. And however near the South came to experiencing the wholeness of life with all its contingencies, as a culture it could not long sustain its life because it lacked an adequate religion. "Its religious impulse was inarticulate simply because it tried to encompass its destiny within the terms of Protestantism, in origin, a non-agrarian and trading religion, hardly a religion at all but a result of secular ambition." (p. 168) The outcome of the North-South war would have been trivial, Tate said, had the South had an articulated philosophy based on an adequate religion; the South — that is the Agrarian way of life — would have won its cultural war, even if it lost the military one. But in the present condition of society, lacking a real religion, the Southerner must embrace political means for reclaiming the tradition; he must become a "radical," in the sense of "cutting away the overgrowth and getting back to the roots." (p. 175)

Not until his essay on Emily Dickinson (1932) does Tate directly discuss the traditional sensibility as it affects the writer. Miss Dickinson is like Donne, he maintains, in having an undivided sensibility; she "perceives *abstraction* and thinks *sensation*." Within her poetic mode, he continues, she "cannot reason at all," but "grasps the

terms of the myth directly." (*Collected Essays*, p. 205)
Tate argues that Dickinson, like Donne, lived during one of
the fortunate times (for poets) in the world's history, a
time when a culture is about to collapse. "The poet finds
himself balanced upon the moment when such a world is
about to fall, when it threatens to run out into looser and
less self-sufficient impulses." (p. 209) At such a time, Tate
implies, the poet can assimilate the totality of a culture
and give it voice.

In this essay he further proposes that two conditions
must be present for great poetry, aside from a great talent:
"the thoroughness of the poet's discipline in an objective
system of truth, and his lack of consciousness of such a
discipline." This discipline arises from "a number of
fundamental ideas the origin of which the poet does not
know," providing "form and stability to his fresh
perceptions of the world." A connatural knowledge, then,
which he "cannot shake off" is the contribution of culture
to a poet. "When such worlds exist," Tate continues,
"when such cultures flourish, they support not only the
poet but all members of society." (p. 211)

Tate's complete "model," by which he increasingly
discovered his principles and the ramifications of his
conviction, was finally medieval culture. His modernism
has thrown some of his critics off the track; what they
have failed to see is that, in being a rejection of the
Puritan-scientific world, Tate's modernism has represented
a return to patterns of thought older than rationalism and
scientism. In the feudal society a communality of belief
and an individuality of function allowed a wholeness of
sensibility to men of all stations. This wholeness Tate saw
as necessary to the good society. The poet is related to all

men in sharing the same view of reality; his work, however, is different from other kinds of endeavor and consequently his formal discipline is unique and not to be subverted, even for a higher good. Poetry therefore cannot be made to serve the ends of religion, nor metaphysics, nor social justice; if he surrenders the uniqueness of his mode of discourse, the poet subverts his work.

Tate continued this concern with the health of culture in an important essay, "What is a Traditional Society?," first delivered as a speech at the University of Virginia in 1936. In this work he makes clear that the limitations of the South were severe; nevertheless the society which defeated it – call it the North or call it Now – had even more serious defects. Tate draws a chart to illustrate the decline of sensibility:

> First, there is the religious imagination, which can mythologize indiscriminately history, legend, trees, the sea, animals, all being humanly dramatized, somehow converted to the nature of man. Secondly there is the historical imagination, which is the religious imagination *mdnque'* – an exercise of the myth-making propensity of man within the restricted realm of historical event . . . The third stage is the complete triumph of positivism. (*Collected Essays*, p. 298)

The Old South possessed the historical imagination, Tate maintains, and though this was only an imitation of the religious, it could at least allow its economic and social life to be unified. In contrast, a completely "positivistic" society views work as drudgery from which social life is an escape. In losing both the higher and lower myth, Tate warns, a society loses "the forms of human action"; and the decay of morality, religion, manners leaves a people

with an "inexhaustible vitality" which they express in vio-
lence and chaos. This chaotic behavior is the mark of the
untraditional society, which can bequeath nothing from
one generation to another. What is passed on in a
traditional society, Tate believes, is a moral vision,
contained within a code of manners and symbolized by the
heritage of a body of property; for "the economic basis of
life is the soil out of which all the form, good or bad, of
our experience must come." (p. 304) And therefore in the
traditional society based on the land, "men do not have to
put aside their moral natures." "Traditional men are never
quite making their living, and they never quite cease to
make it." (p. 303) A traditional society, then, is not
simply one with a past; if such a society came into being in
the present age, Tate maintains, it would have something
to pass on, and would therefore be traditional: "That
something would be a moral conception of man in relation
to the material of life." (p. 303)

Tate writes explicitly about cultural concerns in several
other essays, notably "The New Provincialism" (1945),
in which he is interested in pointing out the difference between regionalism and provincialism. Alarmed
at the tendencies toward the construction of "one world,"
a standardized society without any local flavor, he
makes the distinction: "Regionalism is limited in space
but not in time," whereas the provincial attitude is
limited in time but not in space." (*Collected Essays*, p.
286) For Tate, people living in certain locales and limited
in their acquaintance with other regions do not live merely
in the present; they live with the memories of their forebears; the past is part of the present to them. But people
who live in a world-wide community, concerned only with

communication, not with what is communicated, are provincial; they do not know that the past existed; they have no memory; they have only response to present stimuli. Tate considers that the modern lives in a society that is being pushed into a world-wide provincialism by "industrial capitalism" and "Utopian politics."

However alarming the present prospect of society might be to Tate, he never really rejects his social obligation. The high calling of the man of letters, as Tate sees it, extends the responsibility of literary critic from an examination of the minute details of individual works to the whole range of culture. Many of his essays have been primarily cultural and only secondarily literary; others are quite directly literary, concerned with prosody, language, symbol, theme, and structure, but opening always onto the larger moral and spiritual realm that is the territory of culture. More than most critics of any bent, however, Tate has been aware of the medium in which he worked; many of his essays take for their concern a criticism of the act of criticism.

In this latter category are such essays as "The Present Function of Criticism" (1940), "Literature as Knowledge" (1941), "Miss Emily and the Bibliographers" (1940), and "Is Literary Criticism Possible?" (1950). "It may not be necessary to know what criticism is," he writes in the last of these; "it may be quite enough to see that it is now being written, that a great deal of it was written in the past, that it is concerned with one of the chief objects of humanistic study: Literature." (*Collected Essays*, p. 475) Critical discourse is one of three kinds: (1) evaluation of literature; (2) communication of insights; and (3) rhetorical study of the language of imaginative works. Tate maintains that the first two of these cannot be taught and that the third has fallen into almost irrecoverable decay. Nonetheless, there are still possibilities for criticism. He places criticism midway between imagination and philosophy, a difficult position to maintain since it must not replace the object of its attention by too imaginative an interpretation or too explicit an evaluation. Elsewhere he prescribes that its language should be plain, not competitive with that of the subject work.

But all of Tate's concern for criticism and for culture stems from his awareness of the special mode of knowledge presented by poetry. Beginning in the thirties, along with the development of his convictions concerning society, Tate undertook the process of working out his complete view of poetry. His essay written in 1938, "Tension in Poetry," clarifies his limited dualism. He lopped off the prefixes from "extension" and "intension" to make his key-word *tension*, seeing poetry as existing between these two opposite poles. At one extreme is extension, which tends toward "simple abstraction of the object into a universal; at the other extreme is intension, a merging with the object in pure feeling." "The metaphysical poet, as a rationalist," he writes, "begins at or near the extensive or denoting end of the line; the romantic or Symbolist poet at the other, intensive end, and each by a straining feat of the imagination tries to push his meanings as far as he can towards the opposite end so as to occupy the entire scale." *(Collected Essays,* p. 86)

As early as 1936 Tate was writing (in his preface to *Reactionary Essays on Poetry and Ideas*) that poetry does not "explain" our experience. It is "at once more modest and, in the great poets, more profound. It is the art of apprehending and concentrating our experience in the mysterious limitations of form." (p. xv) Tate's word for Ransom's ontological *order* is *form*; and it is this sense of form that is at the base of his criticism. And for Tate, form is knowledge, a special kind of knowledge that cannot be expressed in any other way. In "Narcissus as Narcissus" (1938) he writes: "If the poem is a real creation it is a kind of knowledge that we did not possess before. It is not knowledge about something else; the poem is the fulness of that knowledge." (p. 250) And in "The Present Function of Criticism" (1940):

> The function of criticism should have been in our time as in all times to maintain and to demonstrate the special, unique, and complete knowledge which the greatest forms of literature afford us. And I mean quite simply knowledge, not historical documentation and information. (p. 8)

The greatest critical insight toward which all of Tate's work has been leading is contained in two seminally important essays: "The Symbolic Imagination" and "The Angelic Imagination," both written in 1951. Dante had long been Tate's exemplar for the true poet: given the forms of experience by his society, Dante was free in a way that no poet has been since. In contrast, Poe had begun to represent for Tate (in his essay "Our Cousin, Mr. Poe," 1949) the disjunction of the modern, in his peculiar anesthesia of the senses and hypertrophy of the will. Tate found the difference in the two poets to lie in the kind of imagination each possessed, the way in which each "saw" his world and attempted to combine his vision and his perception in a unity.

In "The Symbolic Imagination," Tate is concerned to
show how the medieval poet's vision ascended, by a chain
of analogies, into the region of the transcendent, beginning
with an image of Beatrice. The poet, according to Tate,
must turn his gaze upon something in the physical order
and see in this actual object, person, or action a series of
analogies to the metaphysical order; but he must go
through the finite to reach this transcendence.

> To bring together various meanings at a single
> moment of action is to exercise what I shall speak
> of here as the symbolic imagination; but the line of
> action must be unmistakable, we must never be in
> doubt about what is happening; for at a given stage
> of his progress the hero does one simple thing, and
> one only. The symbolic imagination conducts an
> action through analogy, of the human to the
> divine, of the natural to the supernatural, of the
> low to the high, of time to eternity. (p. 412)

The poet cannot circumvent this passage through the
physical; if he seeks for essence, for an immediate intuition
of being, he is exercising what Tate calls the "angelic
imagination." Tate sees this disease of the imagination as
having arisen during the seventeenth century, at the time
when the human intellect denied its limitations and set
itself up in "quasi-divine independence."

The Divine Comedy, in contrast to much modern
poetry, then, is a poem of vision, but one that starts with
the simplest things, with the ordinary objects and actions
of human experience. Tate fears that the poet in our time,
even the Catholic poet, no longer has this kind of entrance
into nature; our abstract thinking has cut us off from
participation in the physical order of being.

This ultimate form of hybris is most fully explicated in "The Angelic Imagination," written in the same year as "The Symbolic Imagination" and two years after "Our Cousin, Mr. Poe" (1949). In this essay, subtitled "Poe as God," the romantic Southern poet is taken as a transitional man, representing a horror of diseased perception which he has anticipated: it is what we shall all come to, Tate warns, unless we accept our lot as creatures. Poe was a religious man, Tate contends, whose religion was distorted by the "fragmented provincial theologies" which he inherited. His failure to achieve any sort of harmony within himself "resulted in a hypertrophy of the three classical faculties: feeling, will, and intellect." (*Collected Essays*, p. 434) What Poe has done, finally, Tate argues, is to "circumvent the natural world and try to put himself not in the presence of God, but in the seat of God." (p. 453) Unlike Dante, Poe has not carried anything physical along with him — in his heart and imagination — as he has climbed to the top of the ladder. Consequently when he arrives at the summit of insight, he can see nothing. "Poe as God sits silent in darkness," Tate writes. "Man as angel becomes a demon who cannot initiate the first motion of love, and we can only feel compassion with his suffering, for it is potentially ours." (p. 454)

Tate's powerful insight into angelism informs all his criticism in one way or another. It is this presence of a negative force or a solipsism within poetry and culture which he has always discerned most vividly. As he has remarked in *Reason and Madness* (1941), he has been concerned in his critical writing with "a deep illness of the modern mind," with man suffering from unbelief; he has seen the mind as "the dark center from which one may see

coming the darkness gathering outside us." Tate's
understanding of his vision has not changed. In his essay
"The Man of Letters in the Modern World" (1952) he
most fully defines his critical stance — one which is
unsparing in its assertion of the critic's task of
discrimination and judgment in this era of mass
communication. In Tate's view the modern illness stems
from the secularization of culture, which has produced,
"the society of means without ends, in which nobody
participates with the full substance of his humanity."
(*Collected Essays*, p. 385) It is this society, Tate continues,
in which everybody acts his part . . . in the plotless drama
of withdrawal." And, within this disintegration the jargon
of communication urges a false unity; for if men were not
each hopelessly separated from one another, there would
be no need of communication to bridge isolated
consciousnesses. Tate proposes that the only valuable
communication is actually a communion — an act of
participation rather than an isolated transfer of data — the
former being achieved most fully in literature. In this
communion men acknowledge the common ground of
human experience:

> Perhaps it is not too grandiose a conception to
> suggest that works of literature, from the short
> lyric to the long epic, are the recurrent discovery
> of the human communion as experience in a
> definite place and at a definite time. (p. 388)

Literature, as Tate sees it, is a mode of knowledge that is
unique and invaluable, and thus the task of the man of
letters is to be a guardian of the language as it has been
given form in literature, to "keep alive the knowledge of
ourselves" which only the literary arts can provide. Tate's

allegiance to this purpose informs his exercise as a critic; and though it requires him to be merciless in his discernment of the false image of man which the modern era projects, still his critical viewpoint grows out of his hope in the communal order in which man can participate through literature:

> It is the duty of the man of letters to supervise the culture of language, to which the rest of culture is subordinate, and to warn us when our language is ceasing to forward the ends proper to man. The end of social man is communion in time through love, which is beyond time. (p. 393)

The least-known Fugitive critic, DONALD DAVIDSON, was nonetheless one of the vital forces in the movement, fully as original as Ransom and Tate and on many issues hardly less important. In his friendship with these literary allies, Davidson tended to play the more pliant part, giving their work his passionate attention and respect even when at times he differed with its direction. He was less theoretical, less ironic, less "modern" than his two colleagues, more loyal to the actualities that he knew, faithful all his life to his particular heritage, though in no sense narrowly provincial in outlook. As poet, critic, historian, and teacher, Davidson came to espouse a conception of poetry as an essentially oral tradition, expressive of the experience of a community and needed by' it for identity and, finally, survival. Thus he has regarded the poetic imagination as properly operative in the whole of society, producing only at times the embodied poem, which may or may not be committed to writing. But always in his view poetry should give form to communal experience and, by operating within society, be in a sense ratified by it; for thus, having gained a kind of consensus, it is able to consolidate and preserve the tradition among men.

Davidson was born August 18, 1893, in Campbellsville, Tennessee, and attended a private preparatory school before entering Vanderbilt in 1909. His father was a schoolmaster, his mother a music teacher; and the literary and lyrical influence which they embodied was not wasted on the boy. Nor were the tales of his pioneer forebears who, four generations before, had been the first to set plow into virgin soil. Family lore made evident to Davidson the presence of his own past. and omnivorous early reading extended his sense of a continuity throughout Western history.

One of the chief themes of the New Critics, as R. W. Stallman has pointed out, has been the loss of tradition in the modern world. A distinguishing feature of Davisdon's criticism has been his emphasis on its stubborn presence. Perhaps this dissimilarity of outlook is due to his essentially different conception of tradition. To T. S. Eliot, for instance, tradition is a coherent set of truths expressed primarily in great literature and subject to recall by recreation in the minds of men; to Yeats it has been a body of occult symbols at the core of the world's knowledge, archetypes that must be discovered over and over again. Both of these views assume a kind of elitism. In contrast, the Southern critics have conceived of tradition as the property of society as a whole. Ransom has seen it as a symbolic construct made by men in piety toward their myths, confronted by the inscrutability of nature and the terror of a God who cannot be understood. For Tate it means the magnificent hypostasis of right order laboriously put together by Western man within the classical-Christian world and available as paradigm or sacrament. But for Davidson, tradition consists of something quite real within men themselves when they have lived together as a community — a residue of norms, values, and memories that is imperishable. These feelings and attitudes are not merely behavioral in origin; they are the gifts of a "just and merciful God," who, as Davidson wrote in his poem "Lee in the Mountains," crowns man's efforts by measuring out "the grace by which we live"; consequently tradition is still alive and available to "all generations of the faithful heart." Ultimately Davidson's vision has rested on his belief in the goodness of the human enterprise, in the virtues which are beyond the power of men's destructiveness. To point this out is to go somewhat against apparent evidence, for Davidson has seemed to many to be the most darkly pessimistic and bitter of all the Fugitive-Agrarians. Paradoxically, his fierce attacks on what he has considered error are traceable to his conviction that men possess right order within themselves and can be called back to reverence for the verities.

Not only in his view of poetry as tradition, but in his conception of the necessary relation between what he calls "high" art and folk art, in his insistence on the need for regional or sectional ties for a writer, and in his defense of the straightforwardly committed lyric and heroic voice as opposed to the obscure "guarded style" of the modern, Davidson has clarified concepts that no other critic in our time has considered.

Several of Davidson's early essays concern the dilemma of the Southern writer in confronting his past. The first of these articles, "The Artist as Southerner," in the May 1926, *Saturday Review of Literature* indicates attitudes that are to make up part of Davidson's permanent position. He laments the "forbidding situation" of the Southern writer, who is at once out of step with the trends of thought scorning the Southern heritage and yet ashamed to endorse a backward-seeming culture by using its materials in his art. He points out, however, that if the Southern writer cannot draw upon explicit local subject matters in his work, he can at least adopt Southern qualities: "exuberance, sensitiveness, liveliness of imagination, warmth and flexibility of temper" — can, that is, abjure the tone of disillusion and cynicism natural to the displaced person. Even the religious fundamentalism of the South, Davidson points out, represents a "moral seriousness" and a "fierce clinging to poetic supernaturalism" that the writer should be able to adapt to artistic purposes. Himself a lyric poet, Davidson felt keenly the absence of a subject matter natural to him — a matter to which he could devote himself wholeheartedly and unselfconsciously. And one senses in these early essays that he has not yet worked out the basis for his defense of Southern culture. Soon, however, his position as editor of the Nashville *Tennessean Book Review and Literary Page* was to give him an opportunity to scan the Southern literary scene in the context of the national situation and to convince him of the worth of much current Southern writing precisely because of the wealth and complexity of its cultural origin.

Davidson's understanding of the South and his eventual formulation of a social philosophy found its true beginning with his Agrarian allegiance; for in his analysis of

industrialism and its implications, he began to see, like
Ransom and Tate, the real battle fought by the South and
the way of life which was still to be championed. In his
contribution to the Agrarian volume, "A Mirror for
Artists," Davidson raises the question of the dubious
position of the arts in an industrial society with simple
material comfort as its final end. In such a society, he
contends, art serves the purpose of merely giving pleasure:
"When material prosperity has finally become permanent,
when we are all rich, when life has been reduced to some
last pattern of efficiency, then we shall all sit down and
enjoy ourselves" (p. 28); and art, being one of the ways of
enjoyment, will be provided. Yet in reality, Davidson
points out, art cannot so simply come into being in such a
non-culture; for by the time of the complete
transformation of society by technology, "there will be no
arts left to foster; or, if they exist at all, they will flourish
only in a diseased and disordered condition." (p. 29)
Industry will then be in "the embarrassing position of
having to patronize an art that secretly hates [it] and calls
[it] bad names"; for art, focusing on the spiritual aspects
of human nature, is bound to expose the degraded place of
man within a wholly materialistic and secular world. And
finally, therefore, the arts will be "extinguished" in such
society through lack of necessary roots for growth.

Why does this need to be true? With money, means, and
methods provided by a technical society, with efficient
communication, and distribution such as the world has
never known, cannot the arts benefit? But we seem to
forget, Davidson reminds us, that bad art can be
distributed more easily than good art. The vulgarity of the
mass media testifies to the terrible communicability of

trivia. Nor can education alone produce taste and judgment; good art cannot be produced at will at the command of a secular society, when the humanistically educated person feels himself out of step with his world.

Within this situation the alienated artist either deserts his world and writes about the past or writes for an ever-diminishing audience and, finally, for himself, with a set of peculiar ideas, private feelings, and an obscure style. Or worse, perhaps, the artist may simply join the establishment and corrupt his art. But in any event the plight of the artist is dire in a community that worships its own technological success and imposes its criteria on all alike. The only real hope for the artist in such a situation is nothing short of "the remaking of life itself" − not simply the technical practice of his art.

The remaking of life itself, for Davidson, meant an act of piety: the re-creation of the virtues, by means of celebrating a specific way of life rather than promulgating abstract causes. Most of his essays in the thirties are on the same theme: the importance of sectionalism for the artist and the necessity of defending the agrarian life before its complete disappearance. In 1938 Davidson brought together eighteen essays on this theme in his volume *The Attack on Leviathan*. The geographical sections in American life are "real entities, not sentimental fictions," he maintains in his introduction. They have grown out of "the accidents and purposes that have attended the adaptation of a people . . . to life upon the North American continent." Yet the sections are in danger of being destroyed by the monstrous Leviathan of uniformity engendered by an abstract and bureaucratic industrialism.

In the first essay, "Regionalism in the Arts," Davidson

describes a counter-spirit of localism that has sprung up in various parts of America as a "retreat from the artistic leviathanism of the machine age, symbolized by the domination of New York during the Nineteen-twenties." In another important chapter, "The Southern Poet and his Tradition," he continues his exploration of the effect of a sense of place on the artist. A "delocalized vaguely cosmopolitan society" teaches the artist no noble virtues," he argues; "rather, contempt, suspicion, disillusionment" are the marks of his cosmopolitanism. (p. 342) Southern poets should fare differently, Davidson contends. And yet, for all the opportunities that they have for acquiring a tradition, they seem to have no better sense of identity than other writers.

> One ought to be able to say of it [the South] as AE said of Ireland, that it is a good field for the arts, especially for poetry, simply because, in contrast to progressive America, it has been defeated and poor and behind the times; or furthermore because it offers its people belief rather than doubt, conviction rather than skepticism, loyalty rather than distrust. (p. 343)

For some reason, however, the Southern tradition in which writers have participated "has been discredited and made artistically inaccessible . . . ." The situation for the arts is so desperate in our time, Davidson maintains, that the artist must oppose the march of industrialism and ally himself with the agrarian tradition.

In *Still Rebels, Still Yankees* (1957), a collection of essays written in the nineteen years after *The Attack on Leviathan*, Davidson has modified his position about the Southern writer, viewing him now as possessing a usable if unconscious advantage. He has come to see the Southern issues now in a larger context and views the contemporary situation through an essentially historical perspective. In attempting to find the deeply rooted cause of the peculiar cultural phenomena of the modern era, he uncovers a few fundamental principles which define the tradition and likewise develops his thesis that a total commitment to scientific truth in our time has threatened the vitality and currency of traditional modes of knowledge. In his insistent defense of tradition as "the great vital continuum of human experience," that is, as a knowledge not merely thought, but lived and reenacted in memory, Davidson demonstrates his wholly unique stance among his contemporaries. The central essays in this volume all explore in different ways his assertion that a culture in its completeness contains and reveres a sacred deposit of truth which is felt as a common, vital body of belief rather than as the purely intellectual possession of artists and thinkers. In the first of these essays, "Poetry as Tradition," Davidson examines the contemporary status of traditional knowledge through a consideration of the position of poetry in the modern era. Since, in its univocal approach to truth, society has adjudged poetic cognition as valueless, the twentieth-century poet has found himself estranged from the community that should provide his source of sustenance. In this position he must become also a literary critic, in order to defend his utterance as a "truthful" statement of experience to a hostile or disdainful regime. He knows that this widespread rejection of poetry as a serious activity is "the sign that the civilization is preparing its own doom." And thus in prophesying catastrophe the modern poet invokes the poet's curse against those who adopt a wholly pragmatic attitude toward life.

Yet, Davidson maintains, despite a brilliant defense the poet-critic has failed to provide a convincing justification for his work, primarily because he has not recognized the traditional nature of poetry as a vital knowledge not confined to the printed page. And, anxious to win acceptability from the skeptics, the critic and poet have collaborated in promoting the "guarded style" — ironic and oblique — in an attempt to purge poetry of any trace of sentimentality or overt emotion and thus to establish the objective nature of poetic statement:

> The style has the distortion peculiar to modern art. The metrical system is shattered into dissonance or avoided altogether. "Prose effects" are deliberately cultivated, in some extreme instances typographical oddities are used to accent the pattern of dissonance, of divergence from the traditional. "Poeticisms" and "clichés" are avoided. Metaphor becomes intricately symbolic; and its closely woven inferential and referential scheme, worked into both the texture and the structure of the poem, puts a severe tax upon the most devoted reader's attention. The poem must be pondered like a problem; it is not made to be read aloud, but must be studied in secluded contemplation. (p. 7)

Yet the hazard of the guarded style is that it can have no real audience except an academic one; created out of a purely literary fabric, it is inaccessible except in the book and must be studied in "voiceless seclusion."

In contrast, "preliterary" poetry, arising in a culture in which the literary art is not yet severed from its associations with "oral narrative and practical song," is "not only the poetry of tradition," Davidson writes. "It is tradition itself." Poetry then as a mode of knowledge, as tradition, is in Davidson's view vital only so long as it is allied with the voice and with memory. Poetry as literature has lost the great communal forms: the epic and narrative poetry, based on memory given oral embodiment; poetic drama, relying on spoken language as gesture; and finally the lyric as song, closely allied with music. The position of modern poetry, then, as Davidson sees it, is dire:

> A poetry that puts itself in a position not to be recited, not to be sung, hardly ever to be read aloud from the page where it stands, and almost never to be memorized, is nearing the danger edge of absurdity. It cannot become tradition in the larger sense. (pp. 21-22)

It is necessary, Davidson asserts, for poetry again to be free of the confines of the page; for if civilization is to survive, it must have available the imperishable wisdom of poetry.

Davidson's concern with the origin and life of poetry in a culture is extended in "Yeats and the Centaur," in which he explores the implications of the Irish poet's famous dictum that "all art should be a Centaur finding in the popular lore its back and strong legs." This unity between the sophisticated and the popular arts Davidson finds to be obtainable only in a culture in which there is an easy transmission of thought and attitude between its higher and lower levels. The low art or popular lore properly has a dynamic relationship to the high art of a nation. It is an existing subject matter which is seeking a formal utterance; and thus the high art is the most fully realized formal expression of a vital subject. But "when the 'high art' and the 'low art' of a nation or a society are out of proper relationship with each other," Davidson maintains, "the 'high art' becomes too 'arty' and the 'low art' too 'low.' " (p. 26) He goes on to point out that; as in Yeats' grotesque image of art as a Centaur, the unity between art and popular lore in modern poetry has become monstrous. The high art and low art of society in our day are as disparate as the intelligent and bestial parts of a centaur, and both portions of the culture's poetic tradition suffer from the deformity.

In the same volume Davidson has a superb analysis of the use made in Hardy's novels of the popular materials of balladry. And he continues investigating an aspect of the same topic in his essay "Why the Modern South Has a Great Literature." It is the organic connection with the vital roots of his community that the Southern writer possesses which provides him with strength and a sense of form, Davidson maintains. Further, special insight is given to him — one which comes to poets in traditional societies having ''arrived at a moment of self-consciousness":

> Greece in the fifth century B.C., Rome of the late Republic, Italy in Dante's time, England in the sixteenth century, all give us examples of traditional societies invaded by changes that threw them slightly out of balance without at first achieving cultural destruction. The invasion seems always to force certain individuals into an examination of their total inheritance that perhaps they would not otherwise have undertaken. They begin to compose literary works in which the whole metaphysic of the society suddenly takes dramatic or poetic or fictional form . . . This is what I mean by the moment of self-consciousness. It is the moment when a writer awakes to realize what he and his people truly are, in comparison with what they are being urged to become. (pp. 172-3)

Later essays by Davidson — on the Fugitive poets, the Southern writer and the university, the New South and Conservatism, Agrarianism, Richard Weaver, Allen Tate, William Gilmore Simms — extend and refine his position but never essentially change it. His importance as critic lies in his recognition of the organic unity of the human community and in the structural function of poetry within that unity — something he could not have understood so well without fidelity to his own land and people.

The effect of Ransom, Tate, and Davidson on their pupils and followers has been inevitably a kind of conversion comprehending far more than literary taste and poetic standards. A deeply ethical and — in the large sense — political conviction has marked their numerous progeny, so much so that the entire body of Southern criticism may be said to assume a place for literature within the total workings of the commonwealth. Of first rank among their descendants have been three writers already mentioned: ROBERT PENN WARREN, CLEANTH BROOKS, and ANDREW NELSON LYTLE. Warren was an active Fugitive — the youngest — and, by virtue of contributing essays to both symposia — an Agrarian. Brooks came to a few Fugitive meetings during the last year of the magazine and was later associated with the Agrarian venture in its critical stage in collaboration with Warren at Louisiana State University. Lytle, too, came to some of the poetry sessions, contributed a poem to the final issue, and became a full-fledged and dedicated Agrarian, one of the mainstays of this latter movement. In some contrast to the work of the three elder statesmen, the critical writings of Warren,

Brooks, and Lytle are in the main explicatory, though the range and solidity of their supporting intellectual scaffolding is by no means insignificant.

ROBERT PENN WARREN joined the Fugitive poets as a gifted undergraduate in the last year of the magazine; and, from discussions at meetings and correspondence with Tate and other members, gained a habit of mind that would allow him to bring to the writing of fiction a critical acumen rare to a novelist. Born in Guthrie, Kentucky, in 1905, Warren was graduated from Vanderbilt in 1925, received an M. A. from Berkeley in 1927, and went on to Yale, where he began writing more seriously with the encouragement of Tate, whom he visited frequently in New York. After a year at Yale he was awarded a Rhodes Scholarship and took the B. Litt. degree at Oxford in 1930. He returned to the States and taught at several universities, including Vanderbilt, before proceeding to Louisiana State University in 1934. By this time he had published his biography of John Brown (1929), written a considerable body of poetry, and completed two novels that were never published. (He has since published nine novels, five collections of poetry, a volume of short stories, and numerous books of historical, biographical, and sociological import. His output in criticism has been considerably smaller but fully as valuable.) At L.S.U. he renewed his friendship with Cleanth Brooks, whom he had known at Vanderbilt and Oxford; and the two edited in conjunction the illustrious *Southern Review* (1935-42) and collaborated on several now famous textbooks that carried the methods of the New Criticism to English departments throughout the nation.

Warren began early, in his undergraduate days, to exercise his incisive critical faculty in the writing of reviews, an activity which he continued all through the 1920's. At the end of that decade he composed his contribution to the Agrarian symposium, an essay on the Negro, espousing what he later somewhat ruefully termed a "humane segregation," unaware at that time of the possibility of any other solution (*Who Speaks for the Negro?* 1965). Warren had embraced the Agrarian principles, as he said at the Fugitives' reunion in 1956, as a protest "against a kind of dehumanizing and disintegrative effect" on the individual person wrought by the modern power state. He saw the corrective hope for the present to lie not in any "dream" of the future, but in the "rebuke" given the modern era by the past. "The drama of the past that corrects us," he declared, "is the drama of our struggles to be human, or our struggles to define the values of our forebears in the face of their difficulties."

This attempt to understand the agonies of preceding generations would ally a writer, Warren knew, to a particular place; it would in fact bind him to a profound examination of a way of life, with the effort almost certain to result in a regional, though not a provincial, sensibility. Warren began his attacks on superficial regionalism — "local color," as it was sometimes called — in two articles written in 1932, the first praising four Southern novelists — Elizabeth Madox Roberts, Caroline Gordon, Evelyn Scott, and William Faulkner — and the second, three Southern poets — Ransom, Davidson, and Fletcher — all of whom had a strong sense of location without being limited to the merely decorative aspects of a region. He continued his exploration of the relation of place to literature in his essay for the second Agrarian volume, "Literature As A Symptom" (*Who Owns America?* 1936), and in a piece for the new *American Review* "Some Don'ts for Literary Regionalists" (December 1936). In these he warns that — though it is preferable to alienation — a regionalist commitment can imperil a writer's work, like any alliance with a cause. The writer's sensibility and his critical intelligence must interact, Warren cautions, so that his convictions are wed to his subject to make a "concrete projection in experience."

An essay on John Crowe Ransom in the *Virginia Quarterly Review* (1935), though it contains a long survey of the philosophical history of modern dissociation, marks the beginning of Warren's structural analyses. In it he examines the poetry in detail, finding Ransom's wit and irony to serve no mere "poetic attitude" but to function within the poems as revelatory of a philosophic and religious outlook. A series of articles during the next decade for the *Nation*, the *Kenyon Review*, and the *Partisan Review* continue the exploration of formal principle as key to moral vision: "Pure and Impure Poetry," "Love and Separateness in Eudora Welty," "Melville the Poet," and the magisterial "A Poem of Pure Imagination," an essay on "The Rime of the Ancient Mariner." A review of Malcolm Cowley's *Portable Faulkner* occasioned a seminal two-part essay on Faulkner (*New Republic,* 1946); and pieces throughout the following fifteen years on Hemingway, Frost, Wolfe, Katherine Anne Porter, Conrad, Dreiser, Melville, and Faulkner effectively mark the end of Warren's explication. Later essays on the spiritual and ethical aspects of literature have been testimonial to the metaphysical system lying behind even his most technical readings.

One theme penetrates all Warren's works — his poetry, his fiction, his criticism: the conflict, for man, between World and Idea. The world is that set of tough, incontrovertible conditions that man encounters in his brute experience of actuality; the Idea is the dream, the moral and spiritual vision of how things ought to be. Warren rebukes the idealist and the rationalist for their wilful ignorance of the contingencies of life, which can be given significance only by an act of imagination. Indeed in his creative works he builds "models" of imagination impinging on action, much in the manner of a physicist making visible the structures of experience which lie beneath observables. In his fiction and less obviously in his criticism, America has been the testing ground for the warring elements of world and idea. Warren's concern for the Negro is part of this struggle to bring observed experience into some moral coherence, to "save" the dream by confronting the worst violation of it. It is apparent that, despite his deep concern for form in literature, Warren is basically a social and political critic, not at all a formalist in the sense of one who sees art as constructing an ideal order apart from other human significance.

The noted essay "Pure and Impure Poetry" (*Kenyon Review*, Spring 1943) should by itself provide sufficient evidence to clear Warren of any charges of aestheticism. For in it he sees life itself as giving rise to the various desirable impurities in poems. The idea — the vision — that poetry seeks to express is pure, Warren would say; but the vehicle for embodying that vision must be impure, since it is to be found in actual human experience, with many of its elements, taken in themselves, working against the clear expression of the vision. But the poet submits his ideal to the terrible fires of "prose and imperfection": his values must be earned. Like man himself, like life, therefore, a poem must be impure – diluted, mixed.

Warren's careful and scholarly analysis of the "Rime of the Ancient Mariner" makes clear that this much-discussed poem has a consistent meaning, despite commentary to the contrary. When Coleridge spoke of it as a poem of "pure imagination," Warren points out, he was far from characterizing it as mere fantasy. In being the product of the imagination, the work is expressed in symbolic (not allegorical) form; but in no sense does it evade spiritual and ethical insight. Warren traces two themes which fuse within the work: the primary theme of sacramental vision; the secondary, of the artistic imagination. He finds that "the moral concern and the aesthetic concern are aspects of the same activity, the creative activity," and he goes on to say that this operation is "expressive of the whole mind." Whatever Coleridge thought as a philosopher, whatever he believed as a man – all these are part of his creative act in constructing his poem. Warren draws upon Coleridge's essays, his letters, and various other commentary for his analysis; but, as in all his criticism, the poem itself is primary.

"Knowledge and the Image of Man" (*Sewanee Review,* Spring 1955) describes in more general terms the action which Warren regards as most fundamental to man: his coming to knowledge. Men have a right to knowledge, he contends, because only through knowledge can they achieve identity. The kind of knowledge that yields identity is best expressed, Warren suggests, in poetry — "that is, literature as a dimension of the creative imagination." Literature offers knowledge "of form" — but not, he makes clear, by "sheer formalism." Form is a "vision of experience," "not a thing detached from the world but a thing springing from the deep engagement of spirit with the world." In this essay Warren makes explicit a conviction held throughout his literary career — that he conceives of poetry as essential to the fully human life:

> [Poetic knowledge] gives man an image of himself, for it gives him his mode of experiencing, a paradigm of his inner life, his rhythm of destiny, his tonality of fate. And this evocation, confrontation, and definition of our deepest life gives us, in new self awareness, a yet deeper life to live. (p. 192)

Along with Warren, CLEANTH BROOKS is one of the most highly accomplished textual readers in the language. The Brooks and Warren poetry text (*Understanding Poetry*, 1938) is a classic manual for the intellectual and imaginative skills required in the apprehension of poems. The controversy caused by this book and the battles fought for and against its adoption seem ludicrous in retrospect but were in fact turning points in American education. In its effort to make readers consider a poem wholly to itself, apart from any biographical or historical association, the book emphasized the essential objectivity and permanence of poetic utterance. The process of understanding a poem, the text makes clear, is remarkably complex. It requires judgment, finally; and in asking freshmen to make judgments. Brooks and Warren were flying in the face of long-established practice in college English. But the efficacy of the pedagogy could not be gainsaid; the text and the cause were taken up by young instructors across the country, their dexterity and enthusiasm preparing the groundwork·for the demise of historicism in academic circles.

Cleanth Brooks was neither a Fugitive nor a full-fledged Agrarian in actuality; yet, because he worked closely with members of both groups and shared most of their views (he contributed an essay to the second "Agrarian" volume, *Who Owns America?*), he is customarily associated with them and even many times taken to be the chief spokesman for their principles. Younger than the others (born in Murray, Kentucky, in 1906), he finished at Vanderbilt three years later than Warren and Lytle and received his M.A. at Tulane the following year (1929). He spent three years at Oxford on a Rhodes Scholarship, and, after receiving his B. Litt. in 1932, took a position at Louisiana State University, where he and Warren were to make literary history.

Much of Brooks' critical position is revealed in *Understanding Poetry* and in the other texts following, on fiction (1943) and drama (1947). Fuller treatment of his position is provided by three important collections of essays, *Modern Poetry and the Tradition* (1939), *The Well Wrought Urn* (1947), and *A Shaping Joy* (1971). A history of literary criticism, written with W. K. Wimsatt (1957), a series of essays on the implicit religious vision of several modern writers (*The Hidden God*, 1962), and a critical volume on Faulkner (1963) are entirely different kinds of studies for Brooks, but all three are authoritative, incisive, and original.

Modern Poetry and the Tradition is an explanation and a defense of modern poetry, organized around explications of Tate, Eliot, Frost, Auden, Yeats, and other twentieth-century poets. Brooks points out that wit, functional metaphor, irony, indirection, and complication such as the moderns exhibit have been properties of traditional poetry, although rare in the century immediately past. Indeed, the Romantics and Victorians have done the course of English literature a great disservice, Brooks argues, by thinking of poetry as the statement of some high moral truth, keeping the intellect entirely separate from the emotions, and considering some objects basically poetic and others unpoetic. Brooks proposes a revised history of English literature in the light of the principles of contemporary criticism.

In *The Well Wrought Urn* he develops with more certainty his concept of paradox as lying at the very heart of poetic expression. Bringing together a number of well-known English poems, he proceeds to examine them from the vantage point of structure. Brooks discovers in Wordsworth's sonnets and his "Intimations" ode, in Gray's "Elegy," and in Milton's "L'Allegro" and "Il Penseroso," in Keats' "Ode on a Grecian Urn," as well as in Donne's "Canonization" and Herrick's "Corinna's Going a-Maying," the underlying tension of paradox which in his earlier work he had limited primarily to the Metaphysical poets. He establishes in one essay the "heresy" of paraphrase and in another the fallacy of "communication" in poetry. This volume ends, also, with comments concerning a proposed revision of literary history which would enable the discipline to avoid the critical relativism that has hampered it for the past several decades. *The Well Wrought Urn* is a brilliantly impressive collection of essays, one of the best single volumes in twentieth-century criticism.

These two volumes provoked such widespread attention that even Brooks' allies and friends, such as Ransom and William Empson, were constrained to point out flaws in his methodology, fearing, as they indicated, a "new orthodoxy" resulting from his brilliant and agile explications. But, one feels Brooks' contextualism has been much misunderstood; he has not intended to limit the critic to a single methodology, as his friends and colleagues well know; but he has simply been insistent in his claims that a close reading of the text must precede any other operations of the critic. His recent collection of essays makes this position clear.

Brooks' most cogent defense of the exegetical method is to be found in his 1962 essay, "Literary Criticism: Poet, Poem, and Reader." (Stanley Burnshaw, ed., *Varieties of Literary Experience*, 1962) Citing Aristotle as a formalist critic, Brooks seeks to clear the New Criticism of Professor Douglas Bush's charges against its "timid aestheticism . . . its preoccupation with technique, its aloof intellectuality, its fear of emotion and action, its avoidance of moral values . . . ." (p. 96) When Aristotle wrote his *Poetics*, Brooks points out, he discussed not subject matter, not ethical questions, but matters of form. This procedure seems to indicate that even "a man who has a proper interest in politics, history, and morals may still find it useful to concern himself with the structure of literary works and with defining the nature and limits of aesthetic

judgment." That a poem possesses ethical content Brooks
is quick to admit; but he considers the content to be
apprehensible only through submission to the form of the
work itself. For a poem is

> a constuct — an articulatuon of ideas and emotions
> — a dramatization. It is not a slice of raw
> experience but a product of the poet's imagination
> — not merely something suffered by him but the
> result of his creative activity. As a work of art, it
> calls for a reciprocal imaginative activity on our
> part; and that involves seeing it for what it is. (p.
> 114)

Brooks' volume analyzing the underlying spiritual vision
of several modern authors (*The Hidden God*) came out this
same year, and the Faulkner volume one year later. Both
of these books, at first glance, give the impression of being
concerned more directly with content than Brooks' earlier
critical dicta would seem to allow. Both volumes
demonstrate on the contrary, however, that a proper
attention to structural properties in a work of literature
can lead to quite legitimate concerns in the "real" world:
ideas, politics, values. Brooks has been true all along to his
commitment as formalist critic; the charges against him of
ahistoricism, insufficient scholarship, and "critical
monism" have largely been based on a misapprehension of
his total approach to poetry. Brooks has always been most
clear in starting with poems, not criteria. The poem is, first
of all, successful or not; ingenious analysis cannot make a
"bad" poem "good." It does provide the extended,
concerned contemplation that a piece of art deserves; and,
if it leads to synthesis, as it should, it requires a judgment
on the part of the contemplator that places him as
participant in the mainstream of Western culture. Thus,

even the Southern critic nearest to being purely formalist in his concerns can in no sense be convicted of an aestheticism removed from social and moral responsibility, since in the end, according to Brooks, "form is meaning."

Unofficially a Fugitive (he produced only one poem for the magazine, in its latter days), ANDREW LYTLE was one of the guiding spirits of Agrarianism. Like the other members of that company, he is a man of letters in many sorts — teacher, novelist, historian, biographer, critic, and editor, having taken over the direction of the prestigious *Sewanee Review* in 1961.

Lytle was born in Murfreesboro, Tennessee, in 1902. He was graduated from Vanderbilt in 1925, after studying with Warren and Brooks under the tutelage of Ransom and Davidson. He met Tate in New York while he (Lytle) was studying drama at Yale and picking up some professional experience on the stage. He soon turned seriously to writing and to the teaching of history and literature. His novels, particularly *The Velvet Horn* (1957), have been important in their exploration of the art of fiction as well as in their delineation of the commonwealth of values in which all men participate. His short stories belong in the company of America's best. A great part of his reputation, however, will rest on his supple, sensitive criticism, which presents brilliant examples of explication and interpretation in the craft of fiction.

A collection of articles published in 1966 under the title *The Hero with the Private Parts* displays a good range of Lytle's talent. Three features of his criticism lend distinction to his comments: a sense of the meaning of men's action in history; a philosophic insight in distinguishing the patterns in fiction, particularly the mythic structures that abound in even ordinary situations; an acute and illuminating awareness of the craft of fiction. The last of these characteristics makes of Lytle's criticism a virtual textbook for writers and testifies to his long career as a successful teacher of creative writing.

Lytle has written only a small (though superlative) body of criticism since his early essay in the Agrarian symposium, partly, one discovers in reading his preface to *The Hero with the Private Parts*, because he considers criticism a potentially dangerous activity for a novelist. "The discipline of a craft is always imperilled, when it is being practiced by a lesser use of the mind," he observes. He goes on, however, to reply to his own comment by saying that criticism need not be a lesser activity; as reading, criticism is part of the writer's business; to read well, he reasons, one must write down what one sees in a work of fiction. "It is the only way to explore and develop the first glimmer of meaning which by refraction flashes out of the abyss, that matrix of all knowledge." (p. xx)

In an introduction to this volume of criticism which he says is like no other in our time, Allen Tate makes clear that it is as reader that Lytle is distinguished as a critic. Speaking of Lytle's essays as "creative," "highly programmatic," and as acts of "translation," Tate attributes Lytle's superb readings of *Madame Bovary, War and Peace*, and "The Open Boat" to his "acute sense of the inchoate flux of history out of which the fictional work of art emerges." One must add to this list the recent essay on Joyce's "The Dead," along with the Faulkner essays. But it is in Lytle's exploration of the process of writing his own fiction ("The Working Novelist and the Myth-making Process") that he is most illuminating, showing criticism as a means of working backward from the finished work out into the vast "world" out of which the myth gradually emerges. "The writer working out of some form of myth will accept the supernatural as operating within nature," Lytle states. "He does not take the world as the end in itself. His form will be some form of myth." And speaking of the "controlling image" of a piece of fiction, Lytle comments, "the image as symbol becomes the clue to reading, the means by which all the parts are related to the structure. It is not inert but active, being both root and crown of a particular living experience . . . and once discovered, it allows the reader to read, not read *into* a book his own preconceptions and preoccupations. It also guides the judgment as it analyzes the rendition." (p. 186) Such terms as *controlling image, point of view, enveloping action, archetypal action, symbol,* are not mere tags for Lytle: in his hands technique becomes the instrument for revealing a total vision of life. Thus for all his preoccupation with technique, he shares the concern of· the other Southern critics for the cultural responsibilities of literature.

If the Fugitive-Agrarians have not been simple aesthetic formalists, neither are they as critics regionalists, though they have been fortunate in possessing a regional sensibility. Other Southern writers — William Faulkner, Caroline Gordon, Katherine Anne Porter, Eudora Welty, Flannery O'Connor, to name a few — likewise demonstrate in their works a regional consciousness given the high form of art; and many of them — particularly Caroline Gordon — have written valuable commentary. The Fugitive-Agrarians, however, have gone beyond occasional essays to articulate in criticism the principles supporting a poetic sense of the world that is at one and the same time local and universal. They have taught several generations of students that poetry is ultimately analogical, that it is essential to the health of a culture, that it embodies the most complete knowledge of his experience available to man, and that, far from being a mere decoration on the surface of life, it is the very tradition by which men must live if they are to achieve a good life. Further, these Southern critics have accomplished a major transformation in the study of literature through their textbooks, which make use of principles stemming from their Fugitive-Agrarian days. The myth sought by the Agrarians, according to Donald Davidson, has been demonstrable achieved.

But as for having any single "methodology," any one set of principles, any preferred subject matter — one cannot so easily corral them into a common enclosure. For them, literary criticism has had no specific limits. It has a discipline, certainly, but one that the critic absorbs as an intellectual and spiritual habit; he develops no method which can infallibly produce the results he seeks. Ransom came to be as much concerned with philosophical matters as with specifically literary ones, for instance, but he never confused philosophy with literature. Tate turned more and more to cultural and theological concerns, Davidson to social, traditional, and finally historical matters. Even Brooks and Warren, the masters of textual analysis, limited themselves to the text only for set purposes, such as pedagogical necessity might demand. The Fugitive-Agrarian critics could allow themselves to write any sort of commentary stemming from minds committed to and formed by a noble purpose. Their discipline was poetry, part of the body of learning; their mode of study was the apprehension of poetic form; their outlook was classical and Christian; their concern was the welfare of human culture, to the extent that it could be furthered through literature.

SELECTED BIBLIOGRAPHY

I. WORKS BY THE FUGITIVE-AGRARIAN CRITICS

CLEANTH BROOKS:

Understanding Poetry, ed. with Robert Penn Warren (New York: Henry Holt, 1938).

Modern Poetry and the Tradition (Chapel Hill: University of North Carolina Press, 1939).

Understanding Fiction, ed. with Robert Penn Warren (New York: F. S. Crofts, 1943).

Understanding Drama, ed. with Robert B. Heilman (New York: Henry Holt, 1945).

The Well Wrought Urn: Studies in the Structure of Poetry (New York: Reynal and Hitchcock, 1947).

Literary Criticism: A Short History, with W. K. Wimsatt (New York: Alfred A. Knopf, 1957).

"Literary Criticism: Poet, Poem and Reader," *Varieties of Literary Experience,* ed. by Stanley Burnshaw (New York: New York University Press, 1962).

The Hidden God (New Haven: Yale University Press, 1963).

William Faulkner: The Yoknapatawpha Country (New Haven: Yale University Press, 1963).

A Shaping Joy: Studies in the Writer's Craft (London: Methuen & Co. Ltd., 1971).

DONALD DAVIDSON:

"The Artist As Southerner," *Saturday Review of Literature,* II (May 15, 1926), 781-83.

The Attack on Leviathan: Regionalism and Nationalism in the United States (Chapel Hill: The University of North Carolina Press, 1938).

Still Rebels, Still Yankees and Other Essays (Baton Rouge: Louisiana State University Press, 1957).

Southern Writers in the Modern World (Athens: University of Georgia Press, 1958).

The Spyglass: Views and Reviews, 1924-1930, ed. by John Tyree Fain (Nashville: Vanderbilt University Press, 1963).

ANDREW NELSON LYTLE:

The Hero with the Private Parts (Baton Rouge: Louisiana State University Press, 1966).

"A Reading of Joyce's 'The Dead'," *Sewanee Review,* LXXVII (Spring 1969), 193-216.

JOHN CROWE RANSOM:

"Mixed Modes," *The Fugitive,* IV (March 1925), 28-29.

God without Thunder: An Unorthodox Defense of Orthodoxy (New York: Harcourt, Brace and Co., 1930).

"The Aesthetics of Regionalism," *American Review,* II (January 1934), 290-310.

The World's Body (New York: Charles Scribner's Sons, 1938).

"Apologia for Modernism," *Kenyon Review,* II (Spring 1940), 247-51.

"Yeats and His Symbols," *Kenyon Review,* I (Summer 1939), 309-22.

The New Criticism (Norfolk, Conn.: New Directions, 1941).

"The Bases of Criticism," *Sewanee Review,* LII (Autumn 1944), 556-71.

"Poetry: I. The Formal Analysis," *Kenyon Review,* IX (Summer 1947), 436-56.

"Poetry: II. The Final Cause," *Kenyon Review,* IX (Autumn 1947), 640-58.

"William Wordsworth: Notes Toward an Understanding of Poetry," *Kenyon Review,* XII (Summer 1950), 498-519.

Poems and Essays (New York: Vintage Books, 1955).

"Thomas Hardy's Poems," *Kenyon Review,* XXII (Spring 1960), 169-93.
"The Planetary Poet," *Kenyon Review,* XXVI (Winter 1964), 233-64.

ALLEN TATE:

"Poetry and the Absolute," *Sewanee Review,* XXXV (January 1927), 41-52.
"The Fallacy of Humanism," *Hound and Horn,* III (January-March 1930), 612-19.
Reactionary Essays on Poetry and Ideas (New York: Charles Scribner's Sons, 1936).
"Modern Poets and Convention," *American Review,* VIII (February 1937), 427-35.
"R. P. Blackmur and Others," *Southern Review,* III (Summer 1937), 183-98.
Reason in Madness: Critical Essays (New York: G. P. Putnam's Sons, 1941).
"The Fugitive, 1922-25," *Princeton University Library Chronicle,* III (April 1942), 75-84.
On the Limits of Poetry, Selected Essays 1928-48 (New York: The Swallow Press and William Morrow and Co., 1948).
"Religion and the Intellectuals," *Partisan Review,* XVII (March 1950), 250-53.
The Forlorn Demon: Didactic and Critical Essays (Chicago: Henry Regnery Co., 1953).
"Christ and the Unicorn," *Sewanee Review,* LXIII (April 1955), 175-81.
The Man of Letters in the Modern World (New York: Meridian Books, Inc., 1955).
"Poetry: 1900-1950," *Sewanee Review,* LXIV (Winter 1956), 59-70.
"The Unliteral Imagination: Or, I Too Dislike It," *Southern Review,* n.s. I (Summer 1965), 530-42.
Collected Essays (Denver: Alan Swallow, 1959).

Essays of Four Decades (Chicago: The Swallow Press, 1968).
"The Poetry of Edgar Allan Poe," *Sewanee Review,* LXXVI (Spring 1968), 214-25.

ROBERT PENN WARREN:
"Not Local Color," *Virginia Quarterly Review,* VIII (January 1932), 153-60.
"A Note on Three Southern Poets," *Poetry,* XL (May 1932), 103-13.
"John Crowe Ransom: A Study in Irony," *Virginia Quarterly Review,* XI (January 1935), 93-112.
"Some Don'ts for Literary Regionalists," *American Review,* VIII (December 1936), 142-50.
Understanding Poetry. See Brooks.
Understanding Fiction. See Brooks.
"Cowley's Faulkner," *New Republic,* CXV (August 12, 1946), 176-80.
"Knowledge and the Image of Man," *Sewanee Review,* LXIII (Spring 1955), 182-92.
Selected Essays (New York: Random House, 1958).
"All the King's Men: The Matrix of Experience," *Yale Review,* LIII (Winter 1964), 161-67.
"An American Tragedy," *Yale Review,* LII (Autumn 1962), 1-15.
"Faulkner: The South and the Negro," *Southern Review,* n.s. I (Summer 1965), 501-29.
"Notes on the Poetry of John Crowe Ransom at His Eightieth Birthday," *Kenyon Review,* XXX, no. 3 (1968), 319-49.
Homage to Theodore Dreiser, (New York: Random House, 1971).

THE FUGITIVE-AGRARIANS:
Twelve Southerners. *I'll Take My Stand* (New York: Harper, 1930).

Agar, Herbert and Allen Tate, eds. *Who Owns America? A New Declaration of Independence* (Boston: Houghton Mifflin Company, 1936).

Fugitives' Reunion: Conversations at Vanderbilt, edited by Rob Roy Purdy (Nashville: Vanderbilt University Press, 1959).

"The Agrarians Today: A Symposium," *Shenandoah,* III (Summer 1952), 14-33.

II. BOOKS AND ESSAYS
ABOUT THE FUGITIVE-AGRARIANS

Bishop, Ferman, *Allen Tate* (New York: Twayne Publishers, Inc., 1967).

Bohner, Charles H., *Robert Penn Warren* (New York: Twayne Publishers, Inc., 1964).

Bradbury, John M., *The Fugitives: A Critical Account* (Chapel Hill: University of North Carolina Press, 1958).

Bradford, Melvin E., "A Durable Fire: Donald Davidson and the Profession of Letters," *Southern Review,* n.s. III, (Summer 1967), 721-41.

_____, *Rumors of Mortality: An Introduction to Allen Tate* (Dallas: Argus Academic Press, 1969).

Buffington, Robert, *The Equilibrist* (Nashville: Vanderbilt University Press, 1967).

Casper, Leonard, *Robert Penn Warren: The Dark and Bloody Ground* (Seattle: University of Washington Press, 1960).

Core, George, "A Mirror for Fiction: The Criticism of Andrew Lytle," *Georgia Review,* XX (Summer 1968), 208-22.

_____, "A Metaphysical Athletic: Allen Tate as Critic," *Southern Library Journal,* II (Fall 1969), 138-47.

Cowan, Louise, "Donald Davidson: The Long Street," *Reality and Myth: Essays in American Literature,* ed. by William E. Walker and Robert L. Welker (Nashville: Vanderbilt University Press, 1964).

_____, *The Fugitive Group: A Literary History* (Baton Rouge: Louisiana State University Press, 1959).

DeBellis, Jack, *An Andrew Nelson Lytle Check List* (Charlottesville: Bibliographical Society of the University of Virginia, 1960).

Fallwell, Marshall, Jr., *Allen Tate: A Bibliography* (New York: David Lewis, 1969).

Foster, Richard, *The New Romatics: A Reappraisal of the New Criticism* (Bloomington: Indiana University Press, 1962).

Handy, William J., *Kant and the Southern New Critics* (Austin: University of Texas Press, 1963).

Hardy, John E., "Poets and Critics," *South: Modern Southern Literature in Its Cultural Setting,* ed. by Louis D. Rubin, Jr. and Robert Jacobs (Garden City: Doubleday and Company, 1961).

Hemphill, George, *Allen Tate* (Minneapolis: University of Minnesota Press, 1964).

Hicks, John, "Exploration of Value: Warren's Criticism," *South Atlantic Quarterly,* LXII (Autumn 1963), 508-15.

"Homage to Allen Tate" Issue, *Sewanee Review,* LXVII (Autumn 1959), 528-631.

"Homage to John Crowe Ransom" Issue, *Sewanee Review,* LVI (Summer 1948), 365-476.

Hough, Graham, "John Crowe Ransom: The Poet and the Critic," *Southern Review,* n.s. I (January 1965), 1-21.

Huff, Mary Nance, *Robert Penn Warren: A Bibliography* (New York: David Lewis, 1968).

Krieger, Murray, *The New Apologists for Poetry* (Minneapolis: University of Minnesota Press, 1956).

Longley, John Lewis, Jr., *Robert Penn Warren: A Collec-*

tion of Critical Essays (New York: New York University Press, 1965).

——————————————, *Robert Penn Warren* (Austin: Steck-Vaughn, 1969).

Mary Janet, Sister, "Poetry as Knowledge in the New Criticism," *Western Humanities Review* (Summer 1962), 199-210.

Meiners, R. K., *The Last Alternatives: A Study of the Works of Allen Tate* (Denver: Alan Swallow, 1963).

McDowell, Frederick P. W., "Robert Penn Warren's Criticism," *Accent,* XV (Summer 1955), 173-96.

Parsons, Thornton H., *John Crowe Ransom* (New York: Twayne Publishers, Inc., 1969).

Rock, Virginia, "The Making and Meaning of *I'll Take My Stand:* A Study in Utopian Conservatism, 1925-1939," Unpublished dissertation (University of Minnesota, 1961).

Rubin, Louis D., Jr., *A Bibliographical Guide to the Study of Southern Literature* (Baton Rouge: Louisiana State University Press, 1969).

Squires, Radcliffe, *Allen Tate, A Literary Biography,* (New York: Pegasus, 1971).

Stallman, Robert Wooster, "The New Criticism and the Southern Critics," *A Southern Vanguard,* ed. by Allen Tate (New York: Prentice Hall, 1947).

Stewart, John L., *John Crowe Ransom* (Minneapolis: University of Minnesota Press, 1962).

——————————————, *The Burden of Time* (Princeton: Princeton University Press, 1965).

Sutton, Walter, *Modern American Criticism* (Englewood Cliffs: Prentice Hall, Inc., 1963).

Vivas, Eliseo, "Allen Tate As Man of Letters," *Sewanee Review,* LXXII (Winter 1954), 131-43.

Weaver, Richard M., "The Tennessee Agrarians," *Shenandoah,* III (Summer 1952), 3-10.

West, Paul, *Robert Penn Warren* (Minneapolis: University of Minnesota Press, 1964).

Weston, Robert, "Toward A Total Reading of Fiction: The Essays of Andrew Lytle," *Mississippi Quarterly,* XXIII (Fall 1970), 425-33.

Young, Thomas Daniel, *John Crowe Ransom: Critical Essays and a Bibliography* (Baton Rouge: Louisiana State University Press, 1968).

_____, with M. Thomas Inge, *Donald Davidson: An Essay and a Bibliography* (Nashville: Vanderbilt University Press, 1965).

_____, *John Crowe Ransom* (Austin: Steck-Vaughn, 1970).